10699951

The Child's Toys & the Old Man's Reasons
Are the Fruits of the Two seasons.

—Blake, *Auguries of Innocence*

COLLECTED POEMS
The Two Seasons

McGRAW-HILL RYERSON LIMITED
Toronto   Montreal   New York

Copyright © Dorothy Livesay 1972
Library of Congress Catalog Number 72-1352
ISBN 0-07-077431-5
(Paperback) 0-07-077432-3
1 2 3 4 5 6 7 8 9   D72   0 9 8 7 6 5 4 3 2
All rights reserved. No part of this publication may be reproduced, stored
in a retrieval system, or transmitted in any form or by any means,
electronic, mechanical, photocopying, recording or otherwise, without prior
written permission of McGraw-Hill Ryerson Limited.

McGRAW-HILL RYERSON LIMITED
Toronto   Montreal   New York   London   Sydney
Johannesburg   Mexico   Panama   Dusseldorf
Singapore   New Delhi   Kuala Lumpur   Rio de Janeiro

Printed and bound in Canada

Foreword

These poems written between 1926 and 1971 create an autobiography: a psychic if not a literal autobiography. All the people I have known intimately, loving or hating, are here. They have acted as catalysts. But there seems to be another source of poetry, quite outside one's conscious experience. I am not sure about its origin, internal or external. What happens is that one is "taken over" by other voices. As Layton has well said, the poet is a mouth through which voices speak. Does that account for the variety of styles one comes up with? Even within the space of one year I may write formally or informally; in a structured, almost classical style, or in a free arrangement of associations. Whatever the cause, always, I believe, I hear music behind the rhythm of the words. And always one or more of these symbols occur: the seasons, day and night; sun, wind and snow; the garden with its flowers and birds; the house, the door, the bed. Especially do I note the dichotomy that exists here between town and country — that pull between community and private identity that is characteristic of being a woman; and characteristic, for that matter, of life "north," life in Canada. Perhaps we are a country more feminine than we like to admit, because the unifying, regenerative principal is a passion with us. We make a synthesis of those two seasons, innocence and experience.

Because publishing poetry in Canada during the thirties, forties and fifties was nothing like what it became in the sixties — a bonanza! — my books that surfaced had layers of poems beneath them which were forced to remain submarine. For this reason I have arranged the unpublished poems as if they were in books on their own, with individual titles (I delight in "naming" and in finding titles). These have been arranged chronologically, to fit in with published works and with selected work like *Selected Poems* and *The Documentaries*.

To the many who have encouraged and sustained
my need to write, especially my parents and poetry
veterans like Alan Crawley, Desmond Pacey and Fred
Cogswell, as well as close friends still under thirty, my
deep affection and gratitude. I owe some appreciation
also for the financial aid given me throughout the years
by The Ryerson Press, the CBC, the Canada Council
and the two libraries where my manuscripts are housed:
Douglas Library at Queen's University and Cameron
Library at the University of Alberta.

DOROTHY LIVESAY

Winnipeg, Manitoba

Acknowledgments

Through the years numbers of these poems have appeared in *Contemporary Verse* (Atlantic City), *Poetry of Today* (London), *Poetry* (Chicago), *Willison's Monthly, Chatelaine, The Canadian Forum, Saturday Night, The Canadian Poetry Magazine, New Frontier; Contemporary Verse* (Vancouver), *First Statement, Northern Review, Delta* (Canada), *The Tamarack Review, Prism International, Queen's Quarterly, Malahat Review, The Far Point, Fiddlehead, Quarry, Blackfish, New: American and Canadian Poetry, Adam, Blew Ointment* (Vancouver), *The Literary Review* (New Jersey), *Poetry Australia, Anthology of Commonwealth Poetry* (London) and numerous Canadian anthologies. *In Green Solariums* first appeared in *Masses* (March-April, 1933), Vol. I, No. 8.

A number of poems have been read on the CBC; *Call My People Home* was first broadcast in August, 1949. *Disasters of the Sun* was first published as a broadsheet by *Blackfish* in 1971.

Contents

From Plainsongs (1968-1971)

From Green Pitcher
(1926-1928)

Such Silence

Some silence that is with beauty swept,
With beauty swept all clean:
Some silence that is by summer kept,
By summer kept all green. . . .

Give me such silence in a little wood
Where grass and quiet sun
Shall make no sound where I have run,
Nor where my feet have stood.

Autumn

To recapture
The light, light air
Floating through trees
As a river through rushes:

To walk on feet made aerial,
Meeting the grey atmosphere
With one's own colourless wraith:

To feel again the wind
Drawing down leaves
To their last surrender:

To see even children walking apart,
Unreal,
Smelling the day
In brief snatches of wonder!

Shower

Over the wood the rain came running
Like a swift greyhound.
The dry leaves rustled at the touch of his feet,
And the trees whispered and sighed.
Down the rough trunks ran the rain
Eagerly licking the roots:
Quickly he sped through the channels of twigs and dry leaves
And sniffed at the cool, sweet ground.

Over the wood ran the rain,
Panting and hot;
Then on the tail of the wind he fled
And bayed as he caught the scent.

Secret

How lovely now
Are little things:
Young maple leaves—
A jet crow's wings.

I have been lost
These many springs:
Now I can hear
How silence sings.

Fantasy in May

This is a city of tulips
Swaying and flaunting
Their scarlet and russet
Amber and gold
In the wind.

This is a mad month of tulips
Carelessly haunting
Old grey gardens,
Young prim gardens:
Squares and triangles,
Ovals and quadrangles,
Filled with riotous glory
Of tulips mocking the wind.

Candles flicker and flutter palely
On the dark altar:
Candles are yellow and steadily bright,
Trying never to dance
But to gleam palely, soberly, chastely,
In a weak imitation
Of electric light.
Comes the wind—
And pouf! They are gone!
And the altar is black
As an unstarred night.

But tulips!
There is no gainsaying
The will of the tulips,
For the wind blows the red ones, the
        white ones, the yellow,
And never a one
Sputters out.
He may blow and blow
Till Doomsday—
And blow he does!
And the tulips bow and bend
Till each moment he thinks

They will sputter out.
Not they!
Ha! Ha!
They laugh,
They are weak with laughter;
They can hardly dance
To the song he sings.
They totter and reel like drunken harlots
And fall quite helpless
In each other's arms.

Whirr-r! Comes the wind,
Blinded with madness
At candles that flicker and
Flame and
Flare,
That dazzle his eyes,
His watery eyes,
But never, ah, never,
Go out.

Que faire? Oh, there is nothing to do
But whirl down the street like an
     ancient Fury
And leave this city, accursèd city,
To the bands of scarlet and gold.
He will run, he will run,
We shall see him running
To some little church in the hills,
And there he will blow in ecstatic frenzy
The virginal candles all down in a row!

Impuissance

In the field by the river's edge
I found him
Bringing in the sweet hay,
Lightly tossing each fork-load
High in the air,
Swinging it down
To the gold stack again.

In the field by the river's edge,
Where the wind runs among the rushes,
I watched him pitch the last load
And climb to the wagon-top
For the ride home.

The slow brown horses tossed their heads
And suddenly started
Across the field.
I saw the hot sun
Gleaming upon the hay-load
And upon his bronzed face
And strong, lithe body.

I longed to cry out,
"Stay! stay! I am here."
But the words would not come:
My feet were held fast.
Instead I watched the wagon
Pass through the gate
And lumber along the road
Till the boy was only a swaying form
Against the sky.

The sun lay burnt yellow
Over the bristling ground.
I could hear the wind running among the rushes
In the field by the river's edge.

The Invincible

On ne devine jamais la puissance des arbres.
—Henri Bordeaux

In the dark garden
I hear strange rhythms
Rising and falling:
Deeper and deeper
The elms delve their arms
Into the helpless earth
And suck the young wines
Of spring.

Stronger and bolder are elms
Than blinded men.

Defiance

Cover me with gravity
As you would cover a live bird
With pine needles.
Cover me so
And I shall go on laughing,
Breathing the sweet scent,
Brushing the needles away from my face.

O cover me with gravity:
Unless I am smothered—
Wings beaten—
I shall laugh still.

Enigmas

Gloves
As ruddy brown
As oak-leaves, fallen,
Lay on the floor
In twisted
Leaf-shapes.

Did they mean
Surrender?
Challenge?
Or a little wind of anger
Blown to terrify
Mere man?

Wraith

Hold me, hold me,
For I shall go soon:
Swiftly as the autumn,
More quiet than the moon.

Hold me, hold me,
For you shall know soon
The aching sorrow of dead leaves
Frozen by the moon.

The Forsaken

I found a stone
Grey with water's passion:
I found a stone
And was still.

In every hill and valley
Of my contemplation
Stones lay in heaps
In quivering, jagged piles,
Grey with the kiss of wind
And the sweep of water.

I found a stone
And was shaken, suddenly,
Discovering myself.

Reality

Encased in the hard, bright shell of my dream,
How sudden now to wake
And find the night still passing overhead,
The wind still crying in the naked trees,
Myself alone, within a narrow bed.

Explanation

The terrible animal
Pain
Crouched low,
Ready to spring.

I could see his fangs
And his sombre eyes
Gleaming.

It was for this,
And no other reason,
I turned in the darkness—
And died.

Fireweed

Seed of the fire
Sprung from charred ground
To hide the dry, stark trees
Carved in black nakedness.

Tongues of fire on fire,
Where moths unsinged
Seek honey in their need
And their desire.

Flower of rocky land
Growing in engine-smoke,
Scattered beside the curling rails,
Rooted in soot:

Untamed and prodigal
Flower of flame,
You are forever
Seed of my fire.

Widow-Woman

She should know:
Spring has surely taught her so.
She should feel
The slow, unseen
Defeat of sun
And understand
The tang in autumn air,
The fall of golden-rod.

She should know,
Who sowed the fields with her own hands
And toiled
That they might grow.
She should know
When standing there at supper-time
The starkness of the earth cries for some covering
And far and slow at first
The wind comes hurtling down
His burden load
His numbing gift
Of snow.

The Lake

Go out: go in canoes
Over the still brown water
Too deep for any knowing.

Go out: you will not find his boat,
Nor his long, quiet body
Twisted among the reeds.

Seek long in the early dawn
Among the islands
And the green, hushed lagoons,

Seek long

You will not find the place
Where death came suddenly and laid its hand
Like sun, upon his face. . . .

Go out: go in canoes.
He was not made to answer any voices
Save the too urgent, too insistent calling
Of his dream.

Chinese

Whales are the waves
Bellowing on the shore,
Whales harpooned.
Again and again
The fist of night
Pierces a writhing back
And draws the spume.
Again and again
I pace back and forth
And pull closer
My cloak.

It is a night of slaughter:
But for me,
Meditation.

Fire and Reason

I cannot shut out the night—
Nor its sharp clarity.

The many blinds we draw,
You and I,
The many fires we light
Can never quite obliterate
The irony of stars,
The deliberate moon,
The last, unsolved finality of night.

The Garden of Childhood

The Gulls

How clearly, after these years, it all comes back
As if this moment I were standing with feet pressed
Between the rough lichen and the soft moss of the rock
Standing in the grey glare of light, with a warm wind blowing
And far below me the unheard thunder of the lake.
Then, as now, I seemed to be alone
Swayed as the scraggly birches were, by wind,
My body no longer mine, but something loosened, free,
Yet bound forever to the rock,
Possessed forever by the wind.

Far out on a tiny island
Seagulls had found a habitation
And now in their curious way were strutting about
Flapping their wings, diving, and calling
One to another, with high harsh voices.
If I lay down upon the rock
Or turned for a moment from gazing out
And gazed instead at the grey wall of rock behind
Then it seemed that the voices of the gulls
Were human, piercing and anguished
As of someone lost, calling vainly to another
Then silent for a moment, listening
To the faint, anguished echo.

And all the while the flutter of the gulls' wings,
And of the waves, the flutter even of the smoky clouds
Far above the waving birches,
All these I saw with my eyes closed
And so leaped up, and danced
And followed the motion of water and sky,
Of gulls' wings, and cried out in answer
As the voices of gulls rose and were echoed:
And so, running and shouting, I went down among the rocks
And plunged away from the wind
Out with the gulls through the warm, thundering water.

August (*i*)

At dawn I awake,
Suddenly cold.
Crows heavily shouting
Forerunners of autumn coolness.
Closing my eyes
I see sentinels of golden-rod
In sleep's grey doorways.

August (*ii*)

Now all the garden tires of the sun,
Lies humbly in the dust and waits resigned
Till autumn wind goes swiftly singing down
The arches of the rain. This day is hard
And pitiless, the sun burns on a rose
Destroying every petal, one by one.
Red hollyhocks shake out their bells to mark
The trembling hours. Beyond the tangled phlox,
There at the casual entry of a wood
The ragged flower of Michaelmas yearns out
Towards the clearing. Not a robin sings;
And plaintive silence, like a child grown still
From too much weeping, wearily now rests
Upon each drooping grass, each dusty leaf.

Omens

The whip-poor-will is still to-night
Because of thunder in the woods
Because of storm in many trees
And wind upon the sea of leaves.

The whip-poor-will is still to-night
Because of darkness caught in flight
Uplifted by the storm-wind's might
And pressed against the shuddering trees.

Indian Summer

You would think spring were here,
So softly does the air lie
So sweetly does the sun fall:
You would think spring were here
And never guess
How winter is conspiring with November
To raise its tower of swords.

The Shrouding

Sun through the winter's dust
Gleams meagrely
In mockery of birds who through the afternoon
Murmur their short, inconsequent sharp notes
And think to welcome spring.

For still snow clings
Along the northern fences
Greyish and all unkempt:
Still the elms stand lone
Seeming to harbour winter in their boughs,
Unready still to yield to loosening sap,
Unready for the battle with the sun.

Must we awake from this long quietness of sleep,
Must we arise and find
Beauty in wakening?

Let me lie safe on lonely northern ground
Safe in the snow;
Wrap me in silence, let me not ever know
When the sun burns, nor whither flies the crow.

Old Song

Feed the fire long
Now that the old are dying
Feed the fire,
Father the blaze.
Give to the dying
All they desire:
Warmth and its song
Through their chill days:

Feed the fire long
Father the blaze
For to the dead
Soon will belong
Earth for their bread
Stones for their praise:
Feed the fire long
Father the blaze.

Hermit

They say this earth bears little enough of yield
For all the strength I've put in it: I'm old,
They say, and what have I done but lift a few
Heavy grey stones from the earth, and watched perhaps
A few small crops grow in the sun and rain
Partners with burdock and wild mustard seed?
Gathered small raspberries in a rough tin cup
From a prickly bush or so, only enough
For supper-time? Or picked potato-bugs
From yellowish plants, bound to have little root?
What have I done, they say, to own any more
Than a roof and a bed for sleeping in?
Nothing, on this hard ground. Better go west
They say, or anyway leave your farm alone:
Let the lake guard it—all the rocks of the lake
Lie embedded in its meagre earth.
What have I done, they say?—
                              I'll tell you this,

I haven't been afraid of only a roof
For my head, and a stove to cook potatoes on:
I haven't been afraid of drought, or storms
Bruising the lake, misshaping the pine trees;
The rock even hasn't daunted me, hard
As it is. The rock is old and so as such
I treat it with respect: it will be here
Long after I am gone, unchanged by me.
I haven't been afraid of anything—
—The things you farmers fear: wind and sun
Rain, even, and snow; they're welcome here.
All things are welcome here: men, silence,
Or a crowd of eager boys coming from school.
Take silence, now. You think I'm lonely, yes:
Because, near to the land as you have to be,
You do not feel yourselves at one with it.
You have grown out of it, forgetting that
Man has a kinship with each stone, each tree
Which only civilization drove him from:
If he returns, he'll find no loneliness.
Instead, a silence lifted from the heart
Which in a certain way, bears questioning.
                              There is no age,
No growing old, once silence is understood,
Once death's a doorway back to life again!
One leaf of grass will fall and wither up
One flame robbed of a maple will come to dust
But while the earth remains, and the tree grows
There is no death: life is a constant sun.
What have I done? they say.—Nothing with hands.
But I have turned my face from subterfuge,
I have forgotten the hard ways of men
And what they live by, what they call the truth.

   (How is one to know how to remember
   What masks were worn before,
   When swiftly all walls crumble, and the angel
   Stands naked at the door?)

My angel brings me sure content: a field of rock
A patch of poplar trees against the lake.

Experience

"For your own good" they said,
And they gave me bread
Bitter and hard to swallow.
My head felt tired after it,
My heart felt hollow.

So I went away on my own road
Tasting all fruits, all breads:
And if some were bitter, others were sweet—
So I learned
How the heart is fed.

A Dream

It was as if I stood outside the frame
Of a great picture, staring long within
At a strange country never seen before
Where I myself was walking, all alone,
Pushing deeper and deeper into the sombre woods,
Seeing only the pale sky overhead
And the dark scarlet of the painted trees—
Soon I had disappeared, but following after
Great flocks of heavy birds soon filled the sky
And shook the forest with their mighty laughter.

Personalities

Upon the street, ahead of me
My joy is a lovely whirling girl
Laughing her errant laughter:
And far behind, for all to see
Another grave, uncertain girl,
My sober self, plods after.

Symbols

"You are the house," I shout,
"And I
Importunate without."

A sudden open door—
Too fast,
I plunge to the house core.

In the bare, dusty room
My cry
Vanishes into gloom.

"You are the house," I said.
  At last
  Within, I find you fled.

The Net

There was a beating of air.
Wings flashed,
And a bird seemed caught in my hair
Arrested a moment there
From breathless flight.

I say it was caught,
Its very movement and line
Subject to visible laws:
I say it was caught,
And all in a moment, mine.
I say this because
I knew in my soberest thought
Myself the captive was.

Growth

As children, beauty was imperative,
Although we found it not in hidden places.
Beauty was caught in a wide snare of faces
But underneath, where ugliness may live,
We could not seek. All that the world might give
Of loveliness, whether in open spaces,
Clouded woods, or the path where the hare races,
These we possessed, with a glad affirmative,
Half feeling it was beauty we beheld.
Yet were we now young-eyed, and children again
Would this world satisfy, would this content?
This beauty that only the eye spelled,
Would it be strong enough to answer pain?
From morning into darkness are we sent.

From Signpost
(1929-1932)

Signpost

Spring is forever a question
And no one really knows
Whether to dig in his garden
Or follow the flight of the crows
Led by a veering signpost—
The old wind's nose!

Threshold

This is the door: the archway where I stopped
To gaze a moment over well-loved fields
Before I sought the fire within, the bright
Gold sunlight on the floor, and over all,
Upstairs and down, some clear voice singing out
Music I knew long since, but had forgot.
This is the door, the threshold of my way
Where I must watch the early afternoon
Cast shadows on the road of morning's light,
The gardens and the fields of noonday sun.
This is the door, where others quickly pass,
But where my feet seek out a resting-place—
Balanced for this brief time between the thought
Of what the heart has known, and must yet know.

Weapons

Lest I be hurt
I put this armour on:
Faith in the trees,
And in the living wind.

Lest I be hurt
I walk above the sky—
Taller than Sagittarius
I grow.

Lest I be hurt...
But O what shields, what swords
Can save me, if you too proclaim
My faith, you too invade my skies?

The Unbeliever

What have I done, in not believing
Anything you said;
What have I lost, from lightly taking
Your gifts of wine and bread?

Could I have thought there was something greater
For my heart to gain
By running away untouched, unshackled,
Friends only with sun and rain?

Quiet now in these lonely places
I listen for your voice—
Yet why? When in my heart lay knowledge,
In my own mind, the choice.

Sun

This sunlight spills the answer, and is swift
To magnetize my passion, draw it forth
For you or any man to look upon.
I am as earth upturned, alive with seed
For summer's silence and for autumn's fire.
I am as bound as earth, yet wholly free
As the slow early wind that trails the breath
Of hidden wood-anemones.
I am all things I would not let you know
Save that, in knowing spring, they are displayed:
The softest singing from a thrush's throat
Tells you my thought before I breathe a word.
I may escape—you hold my body still
In stretching out your hand to feel the wind.

Monition

The soft silken rush of a car over wet pavements
Startles me, even. .
Though it is a sound I know,
A sound I have come to love:
Because I await some footfall
The rush of a motor is too sudden a wind
In my mind.

Oh the low cat-coming
Of a motor-car!
It is as terrible
As Fear—surging—pounding.

"Ask of the Winds"

What is there about you that shakes me
With such sharp coldness;
What breath of winter blowing
Retards my spring?

What is there about you relentless
As the March wind's arrow
That makes me tremble and falter
With the first crocus?

Alienation

What was it, after all,
The night, or the night-scented phlox?
Your mind, or the garden where
Always the wind stalks?

What was it, what brief cloak
Of magic fell about
Lending you such a radiance—
Leaving me out?

What was it, why was I
Shivering like a tree,
Blind in a golden garden
Where only you could see?

Interrogation

If I come unasked
Will you mind?
Will you be there,
Ready?

If I come unasked
Will you be kind,
Your look fair,
Steady?

If I come unasked
Will it be
As if a meadow-lark
Suddenly
Startled you as you worked
And you smiled,
But were not disturbed—
Scarce thinking, even,
Of the bird or its heaven?

If I come unasked
Will you forget
What you ever learned
Of etiquette?

Climax

My heart is stretched on wires,
Tight, tight.
Even the smallest wind,
However light,
Can set it quivering—
And simply a word of yours,
However slight,
Could make it snap.

Blindness

You did not see me dancing.
No:
I did not dance for eyes to see.
Only a fluttering breath of me
Flashed with the sunlight on the wall,
Sank—and grew tall,
Taller than my own ecstasy.

You did not see me dancing,
Even then!
Your blindness saves my self's integrity.

Perversity

That day I wore a red gown
Because I could not hide
The warning flame in me—But you
Thought scarlet meant my pride.

And so I wore a black gown,
To prove my humbleness:
But you instead took black to be
A sign of bitterness.

I dare not wear a white gown,
My honesty to show:
You'd take it for a shroud, no doubt—
Uncomforting as snow.

In the Street

In rainy weather
Who can tell
Whether we weep
Or not?

I dread the sun
For his fierce honesty.

Song for Solomon

One day's sorrow
Is not much
When there's grief
Still to touch:

But one day's sorrow
Drops a stone
That plunges deep
Through flesh, through bone.

The Difference

Your way of loving is too slow for me.
For you, I think, must know a tree by heart
Four seasons through, and note each single leaf
With microscopic glance before it falls—
And after watching soberly the turn
Of autumn into winter and the slow
Awakening again, the rise of sap—
Then only will you cry: "I love this tree!"

As if the beauty of the thing could be
Made lovelier or marred by any mood
Of wind, or by the sun's caprice; as if
All beauty had not sprung up with the seed—
With such slow ways you find no time to love
A falling flame, a flower's brevity.

Chained

Even although we mock
Whenever we meet by chance:
Even although each look
Between us is a lance—

Underneath the mask
Something there seems to be—
Some bond that still defies
Our angry scrutiny.

Dust

Again you come:
When I had brushed
Your cobweb image
From my heart.

Again I ask,
What earthly hand
Could ever strip
A ghost apart?

I think you buried—
Turn, and see
Along my path
Your shadow dart.

Time

The thought of you is like a glove
That I had hidden in a drawer:
But when I take it out again
It fits; as close as years before.

Neighbourhood

Whenever I passed the house
At far, rare intervals
Memory stabbed,
The tree at the gate grieved.

But now, passing it daily,
I scarcely remember—
Pain has a too familiar look
To need the averted head.

Wilderness Stone

I dreamed that I dwelt in a house
On the edge of a field
With a fire for warmth
And a roof for shield.

But when I awoke I saw
There was nothing at all
But rain for my roof
And wind for my wall.

Staccato

That must be the wind
Pushing at my blind.
That must be the wind
Trying to force his way—
Certainly, the wind.
Who else?

I challenge the taut darkness:
Nothing stirs.
Then whisper, whisper, whisper—
Someone's trying to speak:
Cackle, mutter, cackle—
Someone nearly laughed.

Phah! It is the blind—
I left my window open:
It is the wind, I understand!
Fumbling at my blind.
All hours I hear it talking, talking,
Like a parrot in a cage,
Mumbling to itself
Words of helpless rage:
Talking, muttering, talking
Fully half the night,
Cackling to a heedless wind
In heedless flight.

A parrot in a cage
And I too deep,
Too slumber-bound to rise—
Turning, I sleep.
There is someone in the room!
It is you.
I hear your footsteps creaking on the floor,
Your breath about my head.
I hear your fingers fumbling at the door,
Your whisper at my bed.
I hear—
It is you!

Crack crack crackle
Creak!
I hear the parrot speak,
Fumbling and pecking in his cage—
Only a parrot in a cage.
The night and the wind,
The hungry pecking bird
Hammer their voices through my head:
The night and the wind
Drown out every word
Your phantom might, perhaps might not, have said.

Oh certainly, the wind!—
Who else?

Sonnet for Ontario

Although I'll never see the purple smoke
Of prairie crocuses without sharp pain
Sudden and sweet: Although I'll never hear
A prairie meadow-lark without a stop
In my quick pulse, an in-taking of breath
Till the wild notes are fallen on the air;
Although a kind of day, a certain wind
Will touch me with old wonder, old delight—

Still there is something in these trees, these hills,
This orderly succession of straight roads
And fields; a sober-mantled loveliness
That quickens with content the turn of years:
So if I close my eyes, there is no choice—
This land grows like a garden in my heart.

September Morning

The mist, a wraith unshakable, possessed
The very hidden parts of earth, the roots:
Until the sun, with slow and certain hand
Pierced gently the pale gossamers of cloud;
And the one tree that stood against the fog
(As though alone embracing on a ledge
A void of clouded light); the tree became
Slowly surrounded by its neighbour trees,
A fence, a field, then the warm steaming earth.
Last, as the mist arose, and the damp soil
Lay upward to the sun, a boy appeared,
His bare feet leaping high from ridge to ridge—
A sudden gesture, like the brown earth's joy
At being free again to feel the sun.

"Haunted House"

If people cannot stay in this sun field
Of wayward grass,
If people cannot live
Where ghost winds pass,
Wild raspberries know how.

Deep in July
The thick down-hanging canes
Bring mockery to the house half fallen down
With roof awry:
Wild raspberries are sweet with wind
And the bees' hum
Around this green sun field
Where footsteps never come.

If people go away
Or even fear to pass,
Wild raspberries and grass
Are here to stay.

The Intimates

"See what the bees have done!"
He laughed, and piled
Mass on mass of blue delphinium
High in my arms.
Blue ran riot:
Mad laughing fountains splashed and ran,
Colour was captured in a snare
Of blue,
And only blue
Lay in the shadows of the grass
And outshone the sun.

"See what the bees have done!"
But only he and I could see
And laugh
And watch the sober-sided bee
Slave on, unwittingly.

Green Rain

I remember long veils of green rain
Feathered like the shawl of my grandmother—
Green from the half-green of the spring trees
Waving in the valley.

I remember the road
Like the one which leads to my grandmother's house,
A warm house, with green carpets,
Geraniums, a trilling canary
And shining horse-hair chairs;
And the silence, full of the rain's falling
Was like my grandmother's parlour
Alive with herself and her voice, rising and falling—
Rain and wind intermingled.

I remember on that day
I was thinking only of my love
And of my love's house.
But now I remember the day
As I remember my grandmother.
I remember the rain as the feathery fringe of her shawl.

I Saw My Thought

I saw my thought a hawk
Through heaven fly:
On earth my words were shadow of
His wings, his cry.

How many clouded days
Precede the fair—
When thought must unrecorded pass
Through sunless air.

Prince Edward Island

They shut out evening from their eyes,
These people of the farms.
They leave the pine-woods of the hill
Alone with their sweet, heavy burden of scent:
They let no footfall beat its music
Against their red sand roads, stretching to the evening and
    the sea.
In among the pastures, that are grown grey with the windy
    dusk,
They do not linger to hear the slow moving of hooves,
The soft breathings of friendly cows among the grasses,
Or the sudden thunder of a young calf, startled
At wind caressing a grove of birches.

And far off, at the foot of the pasture-lands,
They do not come out to watch
The sheer silver of the little creeks that run,
Or wander slowly, softly, slowly to the sea.

O the quicksilver of so many waters
Lightened by the last of day,
Softened by the coming dark!
And far off, the last boats in-coming
To the cold, sleeping sand-dunes
Encircled by the sea.

They shut out evening from their eyes
And welcome morning
With whistling, milking, the drawing of water,
The sound of voices. . .

They know not evening,
These people of the farms.

Vandal

Bulrushes gathered out of the "crick,"
Soaked deep in coal-oil, and bound to a stick,

Bulrushes' flame is the very best
When an old man's after a hornets' nest.

Under the bridge were they! Nerve, by gar,
He'd teach 'em soon what bridges are!

Crossings for proper people to tread,
No place at all for a hornets' bed.

Sleeping-place, haw! And O what glee
Rang out in that cackle of laughter as he

Waved his red wand. The angry swarm
Made of their dying a thunder-storm.

But to him, the old man, they were men burned in bed—
"Hear fellah's bone crack?"—His eyes gleamed red.

Old Man

Now evening falls so swiftly there is not
Anything to hurry him but fire,
Who stumbles on with scythe upon his back
Homeward, and slowly down the once-familiar road.

Knowledge of things was nothing but a light,
The old man thinks, that vanished with the day:
Now that the dark has come he stands and gropes
Each roughened tree beside the gate, that he may know

Precisely where, at morning-rise, he passed
Outward to the fields. For now at night
The shadows make of fences and of shrubs
A world unknown to him, of things he dare not see.

He slips along the lane. But it was here—
Surely it was here the way turned, so:
Ah, here! His feet in stumbling crush the leaves
Scattered in tiny ruts and eddies on the road.

If there is any thought in him, it is
The prayer that this be home, the fear his feet
Have missed the turning, led him otherwhere
Than to the glowing fire, the steady certain light.

And now he draws a shell about himself—
A senselessness; and somewhat fortified
Peers only at the path, remembering
Its firmness in the morning, and his own delight

At seeing what was there, not what was not—
As now, as now... The road will never end:
Things never seem to end, but wander on
Forever through a darkness, through an autumn night.

At last, the lamp! He rests awhile, for breath,
Stares at the strange black poplars round the house:
Then hastens forward, plunging into light
As an old stone will plunge into a shining well.

*City Wife**

Almost before the sun has touched the fields
Horses and cart are waiting patiently
Inside the yard, until their driver comes
To swing with iron hand the heavy gate
As if it were the night he pushes back:
Only to show where slow the daylight comes
With silent footsteps over silent roads.
The gate swings back: one movement, and I watch
The cart, the horses and the man alone,
Absorbed in the day ahead, which means to him
Only the day between concession lines.
I watch: the image of these quiet things
Is graven on my heart. He will not turn;
The horses will not turn, but go their way
Soberly, steadily, up and over the hill
Until there is nothing left to see but hill
And nothing left to hear but silentness
Now that the horse, the cart, the man, are gone.
I know by heart what farmers do in spring.
I know by heart the things I ought to do;
And yet, forgetting all, I stand and dream.

Springs came before like this. Last year the crows
Made all the morning echo with their songs,
Just as to-day. Sun must have been as bright,
Wind as caressing as this country wind.
Yet never, it seems, have I half understood
The music and the singing festival
That cries to be expressed, of early spring.
It is delight simply to stand entranced
Caught in the aery, golden web of dream
The sun spins, while every sense is lost
Within the enchanted pattern of the spring.

Springs came before like this, I say again,
But never before with me, in any year,
Has spring been knowledge laid into my heart;

* A "city" girl, among farm people, is one who, reared in the towns,
comes to make her home in the country.

Knowledge of wind and sun on open fields,
Of silence brooding on some nest of woods.
Why should I know how springs came long ago,
Lost as I am in this? Only I feel
No more is morning like a gleaming knife
Coming to pierce my sleep. Instead it is
Dream into changing dream, until at last
There comes reality—the scarlet sun.
Or say it is song into song, perhaps, until
Harshly the song of the crow breaks over all.

    Jet crows beating their tireless wings,
    Fighting northward where the snow still clings:
    Strong crows breaking into strident song—
    And now I remember how the winter was long.

So are my days kindled from quiet thought,
Serenity, to unexpected fire:
So is my mind a little open space
Free for all varying winds to stop and rest.
So is my heart a wider, new-ploughed field
Waking to hear the slow feet treading there.
Yes, I come always to this memory
Of feet going and coming over the land,
The man plodding behind the persistent team
For all the day, but coming at last to me,
At last to the house, and the meal and the quietness.
Is it to me he comes, or to the barn
Where in the golden gloom the horses stamp
And munch the hay he shakes down from the loft?
Is it to me? . . . But why this heavy doubt,
When everywhere the world cries out in faith:
When every single leaf on every tree
Holds yet a different light against the sky?
Oh, I have followed where the first bare maple
Suddenly turned to gold, where deeper still
There flamed in red a different maple tree
Boldly against the sober evergreens:
And even further I plunged, until too soon
The other end of the wood was reached, and broke
Into a line of pale wild cherry trees

Too lovely to be startled by a sound,
Too young to be enchanted by the wind.

I ran from there, thinking I could not turn
But only follow the swiftly-curving road
Until I saw that silence was swinging back,
A golden pendulum above the wood—
No! the spring sweetness was too much: a voice
Seemed to cry loud and louder: Turn! Turn once—
As long ago one thought he heard a voice
And could not move until he called her name:
The name of all names surely loveliest,
Of lost, forever lost, Eurydice.

> *How many of us have learned, with Orpheus,*
> *Not to look back at loveliness:*
> *Not to look back, lest any evil chance*
> *Should tell us how life vanishes...*

In soberness I walked the road again
Seeming to hear lost ecstasy fall back,
Ever receding as I travelled on.
The road ran through a group of thin young birch
Shining like silver arrows in the sun:
And lombardies, without their summer leaves,
Were free to feel the wind. The road then turned;
Leaving the wood, it ran between two fields.
I found delight again watching the elms
That grew beside snake fences in a row,
Or even stooping in the wayside grass
To see if purple violets were in bloom.

> *Jet crows beating their tireless wings,*
> *Jet crows flying and crying:*
> *How long before they all return,*
> *Afraid of the keen wind's sighing?*

But even so, in my little house,
Even if autumn comes
Will not the dark fall faster then
When my love comes?

Will not the dark bring quietness
And make him forget the land,
Make him forget the harvesting
Of the strong land?

I am not frightened of the earth,
For I have flung myself
Deep in a field of grass and dust
And known myself:

Yet for such long, long hours he ploughs,
Intent on his horses' step;
If I come near he does not know
Nor hear *my* step...

> *Jet crows cawing and cawing above,*
> *Crows in the sky:*
> *Is it a song they shout—*
> *Or a warning cry?*

I may not end my song; evening is here,
And spring is possessing once more the field of my heart.
I must be silent again, as the elm at the gate
Which broods till the time of leaves.—If I speak, will
　　he look,
Will he open his eyes and gaze suddenly into my face,
Starting the fire of my joy, and the sweet unrest?

I hear no answer in the quiet elm,
Still and enduring. Even as the tree, I wait
Till over the hill the horses slowly climb.

Testament

Should Solitude knock,
Say I have fled,
But never say this:
"She is dead."

Should Loveliness come
To show me a flower,
Say I'll be back
In an hour.

For how should they know
Of a thing they'll not meet?
I beg of you, House—
Be discreet.

Assertion

I shall be the dust
That never falls to earth,
The thistledown
Blown by all winds.

I shall be the bright
Atom in the air
Drawn by the sun
Higher and higher.

I shall at the last
Escape defiantly
All your infallible
Laws of gravity!

Fable

I saw a poppy in a field
And could not let it blow
As it had blown the summer through
Gaily to and fro.

I saw a farmer on the road
And could not let him be
Till I had gazed my full at him
And he had gazed at me.

Now must the flower fade too soon,
The farmer turn away,
And I for theft have gained no more
Than on an empty day.

Song for Departure

I went from your arms, to shake
The stars from my hair;
I went to be common again,
To have common care
For the way I walked down a street,
Ran down a stair:
I went from your arms, to break
Joy's fearful snare.

Daedalus

If I should walk lightly again
As the swallow flies,
My feet in time with the rain,
My head in the skies—

Let there be nobody near
To measure my stride:
Let me kill my own fear,
Heal my own pride.

Sea-Flowers

Your thoughts must be the sea-flowers
Unstirred by any breeze
Whose only honey is the salt
Stored up by minnow bees.

Your thoughts that sway in water
Beyond the arm of light
Are cold and waxen and remote,
Drift downward out of sight.

Thus, though they be eternal,
Unheeding suns or snows
I choose the trembling flower of earth
That breathes before it goes.

Journey

This street-car is a cage
Where I sit still
And yearning thoughts
Dart up each sleepy street.

My heart, compressed,
Grows weary in its place;
My bones ache down
Into the wooden seat.

Then suddenly, a stop!
I rise, released
To breathe night air
Like laughter on my face.

Consideration

Should conversation be
What this has become,
A biting analysis
Of one another?

Or must it end
In a placing of words
On little shelves—
As one touches
Delicate china?

Going to Sleep

I shall lie like this when I am dead—
But with one more secret in my head.

In the Wood

That day was a sort of truce
With sun and falling leaves
(We were in the noose,
And both of us were thieves).

That day was a waiting-place
When I lay by your side
And said a little grace
As though you just had died.

That day I will remember
All my days along:
Between September and November
One sudden day of song!

Farewell

A stranger walks now in my shoes.
—So, House, goodbye! she calls.
But I remain, to run unheard
Barefooted through the halls.

A stranger shuts the gate. But I
Stand grieving close to you:
We pluck a leaf, or toss a stone—
Not knowing what to do.

Night falls: so we must turn within,
My footsteps, echoes, where
Your heavy boots go stamping up
The old familiar stair.

A mirror at the top: there you
Regard your own sad face
And think me gone—although I stand
Fast rooted to this place.

Findings

Northern Loon

Some breath of wind from topmost bough
Leaned down to echo it.   I heard
Strange songs that morning shaking out,
Resounding from one lonely word.

You'll turn and wonder in your mind—
Your mood a restless butterfly,
At all the mystery I put
Into the fragment of a cry.

And you, had you too heard that note
Of laughter shattered in the air,
Of laughter splintered into grief—
You, too, had started, swift, aware

Of beasts unsleeping all about,
Of life in every quivering tree—
The marriage never long delayed
Of pain with singing ecstasy.

White Fingers

The room I entered suddenly
Was icy cold
Wind left no corner where the heat might hide
And on the floor a girl lay, shivering.
"Why child!"
I saw the windows open
And the snow
Making white fingers on the floor.
"I could not keep them out," she cried:
"The snowflakes—shouted to come in."

Old Man Dozing

Bright, hard and clear
The sun on the grey pavement.
And I, who am watching people's feet passing,
My eyes bent from the sun
To the sun's reflection on boots,
In among heels and toes—
I grow more conscious slowly
Of the enormity of feet
And the fierce blast of burning sun
Falling on ants
And other such small, determined creatures.

Pioneer

He laboured, starved and fought:
In these last days
Cities roar where his voice
In lonely wilderness first sang out praise.

He sits with folded hands
And cries to see
How he has ravaged earth
Of her last stone,
Her last, most stubborn tree.

1930

Caw

The old crow
Who sits in that elm-tree
Every March snow-storm
Says caw!   caw!   every march snow storm
To me.

He has only to say
Caw, caw
In his strident way
And the snows thaw
The sun burns
And the world turns
Into an April day.

Only a word
And we're all, as it were
Like the bird
Making a stir
Saying "have you heard?"
Longing to whirr
Through the air
Longing to be
In an old elm-tree
Just shouting caw-caw
At you, at me.

Moments

My joy knows no house
It is too wide
For any walls to measure it.
The leaping sun
The flying grass
Can be its only boundary.

As if there were a flower breathing on my heart
Opening and closing
I lie aloof
And know to what tune the earth blossoms.

The Prisoner

These days like amethysts slip through my fingers,
Pale and cool, with a wind ruffling the rough
Brown grasses of the fields.
These days, grown passionless
As the stones of amethysts,
Yet clear, limpid, and lovely,
Slip past as my arms rise vainly
To seize for one instant the beating wing of meadow-lark—
Slip past and fall through my eager fingers
I know not where.
For I cannot follow this falling, nor chase, even
The unseen lark through its heaven.

If It Were Easy

Fire creeps into my bones, and drowsily
I lean against the flame and drink
Succour from burning wood.

If it were easy as this
To creep close up to love
And gather strength

There would be none of these
Cold heavy evenings
Storm-bound, outside the door.

If I Awake

If I awake in the night
Some shadow of the dark wind
That swept my dreams
Trembles and flutters
In a curtain-fold.
If I awake too long
The darkness stifles
So I forget in torture
The cool way summer has
Of brushing pale fingers slowly
Across my brow.

If I awake too long—
Some pain lies sleepless.

And Even Now

When I was a child,
Lying in bed on a summer evening,
The wind was a tall sweet woman
Standing beside my window.
She came whenever my mind was quiet.

But on other nights
I was tossed about in fear and agony
Because of goblins poking at the blind,
And fearful faces underneath my bed.
We played a horrible game of hide-and-seek
With Sleep the far-off, treacherous goal.

And even now, stumbling about in the dark,
I wonder, Who was it that touched me?—
What thing laughed?

Now, I Am Free

Now, I am free
But prejudice
Will creep like moss
On an olding tree.

Shall I then be
My parents' child—
A desperate grasp
Towards fixity?

The Great Divide

My guardian angel, sick and sad at heart
Now turns away his head
And stands beside the door, where long ago
He stood beside my bed.

How I remember his bright golden wings
To comfort me at night
That now are folded back as though to fall
In lonely downward flight.

My guardian angel hears no prayer from me—
I worship earth and sky:
He goes the way of childhood, all too far
For me to hear his cry.

May, 1930

Song from The Multitude

Hushing the roar of towns
And their brief multitude.

—Edward Thomas

They say the whip-poor-wills are singing in that wood:
I have not heard them.
They say that in the cool of evening-time
This June lies hushed to hear the throbbing note
So clear, so golden, of the hermit-thrush.
They say "The apple-bloom has fallen: Mickey has kittens—
Four, fluffy and black; Anna and I
Drove into town on Saturday night in the cart—
Such a blaze of lights! We had forgotten it all:
Winter makes such a difference, closes you in."
They say all this, these quiet trivial things:
But there, behind the words, clearly as now
I see the factory chimney-stacks, I see
The red-brick farmhouse heavy under the lilacs
The gloom, the aching sweetness of June dusk
Guarded by elms and tapering lombardies
And out in the clover fields or the pasture lands
The long thin fingers of the sun stretch out,
Linger in search of quietness, and touch
Caressingly the grass and the purple vetch.

If I could draw a curtain over my mind
As I have drawn so many, many times
A curtain across this city window-pane,
O then I might blot out the memory
So sharp, so luminous, of field and wood,
And never know again the ache to touch
Even one blade of grass clean of the dust.
Then I could turn within, turn to my work
In the house and learn these other narrow ways
Where knowledge is enclosed in parallels,
Street upon street. Then I need not wait
In hunger for your step to come, your arms
To hold me and your voice to hush.

It is not wise for any woman thus to be
So helpless when alone, with no reserves
To fall upon save a blank kitchen wall,
The meaningless ticking of a kitchen clock.
This narrow life, these walls to beat against,
This little space of floor when my quick feet
Would fain run miles upon a country road
Stumbling and falling, yet flying, flying on:
This is too difficult, when yet I see
Crows pressing northward, marsh-hawks crying; and hear
The wary whispered wind scratching the door.
Simply to fight despair, I dance, I sing,
I whirl as if in joy from room to room
And try to show the chairs how gay I am!
But not until I force the table-legs
To caper through the hall, will my dull heart
Be light again, my laughter be like wind.
Not until the mad impossible day
Arrives, when you and I return again
To the wide heaven and the farstretched earth,
And know ourselves through knowing quietness.
Not until then, dear love, will there be joy
To cover us with gold, a sun-like web.

"It is enough," you say, "to be content
To walk out in the evenings under a sky
Far off and cool, and hear the high clear sounds
Of children calling, women singing, organ-grinders
Winding out the old interminable song.
It is enough to be content with love."
Sometimes in the dark, in the night
When the walls dwindle and the sky creeps down
When there seem only stars for a roof, to my eyes
Tight-closed, and you so safely beside me,
No more than yourself, with some strange breath of my own
To quicken the fire that is you, the flame that is I—
Then in the dark, in the night, I cry out, I say:
"This is enough! I need no comfort more."

But let day come: morning shut out from me
By blinded buildings and by chimney-stacks.
Then I am starved for sun, and need
His mantle to go wandering in
And need his golden hammer-strokes
To quicken my slow pulse.

Therefore I say in all the beggar prayers
You do not hear, love is a prisoned place,
Love is a darkness with one blinding lamp
To lighten it, where ever our tired eyes
Must gaze unswervingly, or else we lose
All sense, all sight. Therefore I cry alone,
Let me go, let me fly away, let me find peace
Untroubled by the warring of two selves,
Cool as the dim recesses of a wood.
After too much music who desires
Anything but silentness, any tune
But windy fragments sounded in the grass?
After too much singing, who would not
Forget all words, stand quite still and watch
The silent sun follow the silent stars,
The moon without a sound rise up and pass
All unprotesting through the voiceless sky?
So there is too much passion in this flower:
I am enchained, imprisoned by your words,
Your look, and even less than these—your coat,
Hung upon a nail, which every time
I pass I cannot keep from touching: so,
By little things you hold me from the door,
Bid me to sing within; when some far voice
Integrally my own, is hushed, is dumb.

The Garden Of Love

Again the fever: at last to see you!
At last the deep kiss.
O Beloved, in a café
Hold fast to this.

Quick, remember where we're going
Stumble through the night
Find a hotel, find a latch-key
Any room is right.

"Will this do?" O my lover
Joy, joy with you.
Lovely bed and lovely blankets—
Quickly, love me too!

This day takes hold of me and lifts me up—
Oh ho there, wind!   I feared you in the night.

> *Whispering wind, clawing like a cat*
> *At curtains, sneaking through the window's crack,*
> *Snapping at the trappings of my room.*

Feared you... Feared this? This shivering delight
A laughter blowing back my hair, a voice
Trembling upon a secret almost said?
Never again will autumn startle me
If with such wind, such a haphazard sun
He plays with me, drives sober thought away
Turns plodding conversation into song.

> *But Lucifer came down that night, the stars*
> *Precarious ladders for his feet. He met the clouds,*
> *Stirred up the angry clouds to rain and wind.*
> *Lucifer, the Cat, came down to me*
> *Lucifer, the Wind, the fingers at my blind...*

O subtlety of presences other than
You, sleeping by my side: the heavy dark,
Deepsmelling, and the dream I touch,
The wind a cat   mocking at my safety.
My safety is with you, who lie asleep
Bound in a phantom world to other anguish known.

> *Your breathing is less real than these sharp claws*
> *Of rain without, this gnawing of the wind—*
> *These only, set me shivering in their hold*
> *Naked at last before the earliest fear...*

Yet see sun patterns on the page, and hear
The chuckling breeze that rustles in the leaves
Unfallen yet, soon to be fallen down

> *So Lucifer once fell—is hiding now?*
> *Hiding till night a darker mantle fall!*

Ah no; he's dead! Sun searches out my heart.
Come lover, walk with me
Along the boulevard!

Doves dive up and down
Across our window
Silver and shot amber.

Clouds drift
As snow drifts from hemlock
At a breath of wind.

If we lean out
From the window—
Paris
Irony of Eiffel
Tour Saint-Jacques
Sturdy Notre-Dame—
Under the smoke.

Preferable to imagine:
And to watch only, from within
Clouds, silver-spotted,
Doves, slow-circling,
Peace.

Your honesty
Is a search-light
Small insects
Trembling hares
Cower and run
Before it.
I have seen
A hungry lioness
Scorn—but slink away.
Only the young birch-tree by the roadside
Sways all its loveliness towards you
Rooted, and unperturbed.

I never knew much about silence
Until I knew
Your silence over mine,
Your breath blowing mine out.
Then the night flowed in
And our one listening heart
Pounded the question.

Amazement!
I walk through the revolving doors
In breathless fear—
Hurry! Or you'll be caught...

These are your moods.
Yet I am fascinated:
I must pass through them.

Hola! the moon... Her icy prairies seem
Too still and far to tremble from the dream.

Give me instead the soft warmth of the south,
The rounded quivering that stirs your mouth—

Give me green countries smiling to the sky
And quick, your net to catch my butterfly!

Let not our love grow mildewed, out of use—
Give me your hand, your mouth;
I cannot stay for long in a closet room
Walled from the south.

Nor can I be a piece of furniture
A couch, a chair
You've grown too used to, and admire no more
Its modern flair.

Not conversation, but a kiss must be
The way our breath should blow;
Take me, and hold me close; Love, do not seek
The letting-go.

"Meet me at noon." "All right."
(Letters he has to write).
Had it been me, I'd have said:
"Get early out of bed!
Meet me at eight."—"I will."
(I dream the answer still.)

I am a thoughtless thing—
(Of course—but it is spring).
People at home must flout
Letters to pass about.
(I know, but I have let
Mine be a careless debt.)

Certainly: well I've known
Men need to be alone—
(Why am I not the same?
Is love a single game?)
Don't lie awake all night!
"Meet me at noon." "All right."

Love has come back now like a cloud
And made the world a sober place—
I turn to mingle with the crowd
And find I'm staring at your face;

I turn to run through fields alone
Or seek companions in a wood—
I find your feet before me gone
I am made captive where you stood

No one but I may cry aloud
Or tremble for the sun's old grace
Love has come back now like a cloud
And darkened all except your face.

I am merry; till I lie alone
encased within the dark—
strange womb where consciousness
can penetrate and throb.

I am merry; till like sickness love
enfeebles me; alone
and desperate I toss
with no hand near my side.

and then I ache, for fear that you ache too,
hold the same pain close
because pain has the face
of love, even while it strikes.

It's true, philosophies
Have never darkened me.
I live in what I feel and hear
And see.

Love me, or love me not,
I'll laugh, or run away—
In winter's shawl I shiver
In spring's green cloth, I'm gay!

And watching you, who suffer
From seeing evil crouch
My mouth is washed with silence—
I ache; but can do nothing much.

Dark ways we led each other, though we sought
Only to catch the sun—
A happiness quick shared before the night:
Once to possess, and then divide the joy
Was all our thought. But somewhere evil crept
A twisted thing, between us, broke the blades
Of grass, the flowers grown round us close,
Shattered the laughter that was clean
As morning air, that we had tossed between us.
And so we lost the way—you mine, I yours,
And quarrelled in the darkness— we who still
Were longing to be kind, to do no hurt.
Two innocents expelled, outside the gate.

Shape me to your will:
Since I have failed and hated, loving you
Be with me still
Forget the hurt I had not meant to do.

I found the good was evil, light grew dark.
I found my love deformed against the wind:
A broken thing, it gives no shelter now,
Needs sunlight long before it can grow shade.

Come now and be instead
What I in pride had dreamed I'd surely be:
The root, the head
The laughing branches of a neighbour tree.

These things are patient out of time:
My pen, my desk, my reading-lamp:
I can forget them, days or hours
They still awaken at my touch.

You, pen, to perjure me with words
That only half-say what I meant
You, desk, to hold my weary head
After the rush of thought is spent

And you, my lamp, that light for me
A dark I never learn to know
Because your vigil prisons me
Because mute books will have it so.

I think I have not learned
Not yet
Not after all this living
Love by itself.

I have struggled toward the light
And borne the wind in my branches—
Grown upwards with the wind.
I have lain still in a delicate rapture
I have been wordless before a sudden peace.

But I think I have not learned
Not yet
Not after this terrible, beautiful loving
The way of love
When it goes—
The way to pierce myself,
To run cleanly on the sword.

This denial
That is affirmation
I have not learned—
Love
By itself.

From The Thirties

In Green Solariums

Snow over the city. You don't know the city,
You who sit in green solariums
And watch the snow fall on the garden walk.
I've sat there; I have learned to talk like you,
To keep things pretty and clean and nice; to be
Happy because the jelly turned out right.
Almost I was deceived those quiet days
When the slow fluff fell softly and the trees
Stood dark and stately in the yard. I thought
There must be good in this, it must be right.

"Annie, you'll bring the coffee now? You see
Mr. Hurst and I are going out tonight.
—Thank you. And you, son? Will you come along?
Or is there something else that you must do?"

I waited. The coffee-pot near split. He said:
"I'll wait around a while. And then I'll see
What Charlie's doing tonight. Perhaps we'll skate."
And so I knew. The first night he had stayed
And fooled with me in the kitchen: it was now
Too hushed a night for fooling.—I could hear
My own heart thump. I piled the dishes up.
And soon they went. I finished up alone.
I heard him waiting in the sitting room
And would have fled, only he met me there
Quickly at the bottom of the stair.

O lovely whiteness of you! Lovely body
Young and burning for me. What a joy
To seize your mouth and know your hunger there—
And greater hunger otherwhere.
All winter through the whiteness of the snow
The chill, still day, you burned in me. Until
The dark night plunged, and you came with it, fast.

I've done with that. I thought like that, those days.
Fine words came tumbling out of me, and pride
Lifted my head up as I moved the broom.
Proud! To be sweeping for his likes. Proud!
To be living in a house like that, and paid
For doing it, my body and my mind
For them, my own life bought and sold for them.

Well I remember the spring. A girl alone
Has cause to remember the green roots shooting pain,
The small sick leaves that sprout, the heavy growth
Inside the belly, suddenly made plain.

She saw that I got out; that I was "saved"
By the Salvation Army; that I had no cause
To have another bastard now I'd seen
My sin (and seen the price they made her pay for it).

The son had nothing. A student only he was.
I remember him saying it hurt like hell.
I remember I was almost pitying him—
The twisted look in his face, and the dark eyes.
For a long time I ached because of him
I loved him, you see, and the habit wouldn't break—
Not easily that is; not till I saw
The way those women treated me, as if
Their kindliness had hardened down to this:
Girls come and go; it's the day's work.—But you feel
They're proud because they're well brought up, without
Those circumstances where the sole pleasure is
The worst one (in their eyes). They eat and drink
But do not feed the living body made
By food and drink. They live useful lives
And even see the city, look at it:
But clamber back to green solariums.

I didn't get religion. But instead
I got a hold on things at last. From bad
To worse I went. Lonely it was at first,
And I had a way of brooding; thinking things
Over and over too much. Ready to die
Or go out whoring, whichever came along.
Meanwhile snow came again, and the child was born.

One thing I wouldn't do, was go again
Back to the unreal town, the paper roofs.
I worked in a store for a dollar a day, and lived
In an upper room down near the waterfront.
Snow came again. Men would be out there tramping,
Looking for work. And I knew they'd go
Daily, up to the streets where I had lived.
I'd see them brushing shoulders with a boss,
A sleek, well-fitting business man who wore
A fur coat or a cheerful woolly scarf—
I'd see them begging for a cup of tea,
I'd see them in a crowded sandwich shop
Having maybe a cup of coffee to sip;

And if a man were dirty and unkempt
The management would give instructions: so,
A waitress would be forced to kick him out
Or call the dicks if he demurred at all.

He did not. Nothing else for him to do
But slump and starve and then be hurried off
To jail again—the same charge, "vagrancy."

I was so mad I clenched my fists, grew hot
Ready to fling myself and kick the cop.
The man beside me saw, and seized my arm.
"Say kid! No use. Sit still." I looked at him,
Scornful at what I thought his "cowardice."
But he wasn't a coward. He wasn't quiet at all
But he said, "sit still," and taught me the hard fact
That one lone rebel does no good at all.
"You've got to know what you're fighting against, and then
You've got to show others the way. Together you'll swing
Out onto the road. That's solidarity."
I listened. And more than once I listened to him.
Till after a while it was I myself who cried:
"I have a son who'll be a fighter yet!"

I have a man now who's not white like snow
But who can take me, and be glad of that—
But will not let himself be lost for love.
There's bigger things than love to be worked out;
There's darkness, madness to be fought against:
The men who will not see the only way,
Then men who choose religion or some crank
Philosophy wherein to lose themselves—
These must be battled with before we'll find
The going easy, and the world's new army stretched
From mine and farm, on to the factories.

Yet it will come! I watch the city sleep
And wake each morning with a wider look,
A restlessness of movement, a hoarse shout,
That sometimes hurls defiance down a street.
The time will come. Snow will be shaken off,
Stripped from the trees by struggling fists and arms—
Snow will be trampled in the streets, and more!
Snow will be bloody in the alley-ways.
We will march up past green solariums
With no more fear, with no more words of scorn:
Our silence and the onrush of our feet
Will shout for us: the International's born!

Montreal: 1933

Dufferin Square is a playground
It's a dirty grey place downtown
But there are swings and seesaws:
Dufferin Square is a playground for children.
Hardly anyone plays there.
Along the benches, sitting near the sand-piles
Men with unchildlike, wrinkled faces
Are huddled together. In small groups
They dominate the playground
Solidly round the square they watch the wind,
Swinging the empty swings—
The seesaws point mutely upward.

We must remember: Archbishop Gauthier has spoken:
"Let us be glad that no one has died of starvation
In this country." We must remember
A few blocks away the tailor is making a suit
For Cuba's Machado.—He's not left his seclusion.
Soft carpets tell no tales and the hangings
Of deep velvet bear no bloody stains.

In Cuba the masses have not blundered!
In Cuba the masses know their foe!
In Dufferin Square the men talk in low voices,
In Dufferin Square the clenched fist fears the light.

Why? Why? Why?
Was Nick Zynchuk then murdered for nothing?
Have we no answer for the brutal arm?
Because we live in a city within a city—
At war with itself and its factions
This does not deny the fact of these skyscrapers
Made by the workers—these granaries
Filled with our wheat; these railways shining
Unloading to ships pointed out to the sea.
This does not deny the steel mills and textiles
That we are creating and building
Not separately—Polish, Italian and French
But with all our great strength together we're building.

Dufferin Square is a playground
Where big words sound lovely
But there are words being spoken
That hold meaning and action.
There are words beginning!
There are thoughts being lighted!
Cuba's Machado still fears the street.

An Immigrant

(Nick Zynchuk)

Spring returns again, soft winds caress
The huddled houses of St Louis Ward.
And you return again, newcomer here,
Unknown and unobserved. Over the sea
They knew you. You were a small boy breathing spring
On a bare farm in Poland.
You grew, and starvation matched you, stride by stride.
On a railway platform, barefooted, you saw
Our golden stretch of wheat, our skyscrapers
Embroidered on the air.
It was too much! The sweetness of far suns
Burned deep and touched your hunger: you broke loose.
And soon the ocean's tossing washed your dreams.

The immigrants come in. Women with shawls
Wide-eyed and silent view the fluted towers
Of granaries. They see the mountain's cross.
So Montreal is real!   Its wide shores hum
Its streets stretch into dimmer distances—
Spring is a peasant woman in a shawl
Blowing green mist all along the hills.

Work is spasmodic. Shovel and pick,
One day here and another day there.
Sit on a gravel pile deep in the sun
Munching sandwiches one by one.
"What do you say, Nick? There's a fine girl,
Catch her and snatch her and give her a whirl;
If we can't be millionaires, let's be men!
It's a hell of a country—till you kiss her again!"

The immigrants come in; year follows year.
Slower the wheel turns, faster more are thrown
Ruthless against the wall, to sleep in parks
Or at the Refuge face the lice and rats.
Five years of this now, Nick, with just enough
To live on when you worked; for two years now
You've tramped the streets and knocked at factory gates
That only rattled harshly, and relapsed
To rusty silence. On the wall, a sign
"Your opportunity" is blotted out by rain.
Alert, but empty-handed, the refrain
Comes back to you, Nick Zynchuk: "Years of hell!"

Deep in St Louis Ward soft winds caress
The huddled houses, spring returns again.
The winter's gone, and no one's paid their rent:
The couple upstairs went to jail, and Nick
Here's Nick again, his pockets empty still.
We've appealed to the landlord, then to the City Hall;
We've appealed to our candidate for alderman.
Tomorrow the day is set, out we go, wife–
Unless the neighbours help us fight it through.

Click click click. "Attention, men!"
The sergeant's at his words again.
"All right, Zappa—take this whiskey,
Use your billies if they're frisky,
See? They're bastards, not fit to live,
Give 'em all you've got to give."

The crowd held firm. Then a single cry went up
As the furniture came out. Now working-men
Stood shoulder close to shoulder; silent, tense—
Until policemen charged, beat back, and struck.

Then you returned again, newcomer here,
Unknown and unobserved. What you had left,
A few possessions—trousers, and a hat,
Were still upstairs in an old travelling bag.
You moved towards the door, towards the stair
And scarcely noticed Zappa standing there.
The crowd stirred restlessly. You passed—
There was a roar and pistol crack.
Nothing had happened in the street—
Only a worker was shot in the back.

When spring returns again each widening year
Blue loft of sky, scent of sweet grass hay
Still penetrate the asphalt: wider cracks appear.
Deeper the fissures by the window-sill
And more the feet, parading now, sound out
In wider unison. Alert and quick,
New voices take command; thin children grow:
As willows stiffen in the sun their arms
Stretch out to life; and Zynchuk, smiling quietly
Is part of moving green along the hills;
Is garden for their seed. His breath is blown
Stronger than this March wind upon their lungs.

"Queen City"

Shaped like a bugle
My thoughts, swarming outwards
In phalanx exultant
Singing for these ones:

For you, young lover
Facing the chasm
And plunging head downwards
"I had not the courage."

For you, girl crying
For love had no wisdom
No warm sleep, jobless
No arms to build with—

For you, forerunner
Outstripping darkness
Your mind sharp as sunlight
Piercing our shadows.

For you, sea of faces
Uniform, solemn
Alert for the warning–
Whom hunger outpaces.

Shaped like a bugle
My thoughts split the framework
Of silence and weeping,
Arise, and send singing
This song to the sleeping.

We in a struggling train. Its raw cry rips the air.
The country stubble and the tattered fence flash by
And settle into memory. On rails unseen
We splash into the clouded city's rim, its long
Bare bones stretched out directionless: suburban houses
Spread like playing cards between garages, hencoops—
Children stiff as splinters saluting the unknown
Waving at these our faces, too far off to put
The fear and strangeness in them—impersonal salute.
Now there are coalyards, runways of smudgy steel, and next
The squat and rounded oil tanks with their vacant eyes.
Here funnels fat with smoke from soot-grimed factories
That stare beyond the bridge, beyond the muddy Don
Down to the blue lake water guarded by the cranes
And churned by tugs, commercial steamers, fishing boats,
Oil-manned tankers, flat red barges dull as freight-trains
—O this the expected city, this the dream!
We see a self-important ferry harried by
The flash of life, the wings of diving gulls, cry shrill
And nose in air for refuse and the cast-off things men stuff
Into a pail and clamp down quick the lid.

3

Take off the lid, scatter the refuse far,
Tear down the "WELCOME" from the city-hall.
For you're not welcome, vagabond, nor you
Old man, nor you, farmlabourer, with sun
Still burning in your face. Burn now with shame
Take to yourself the bread ticket, the bed
On John Street—fifteen cents, GOOD CLEAN
And pluck out all the hungers from your brain.

Hallelujah, I'm a bum
Heading now for kingdom come,
Plugging down a railroad track
Nothing's there to drag me back.

Let the mayor pitter patter
But it really doesn't matter
If he tries to pray
As long as I've a bed tonight
It's a lovely day!

Hallelujah, here's a train
Hallelujah, try again,
Scrambling up a gravel bank—
If I'm dead you've me to thank.

4

Peace in the city's heart, O will you find
Peace in this place again? For not the throb of sound
Nor scurrying bodies darting into doors
Should mar your search, philosopher. The drift
Of light between gaunt buildings should suffice
To blot out grime of brick; your thought alone
Should scrape grey walls until they bleed again.
"Such suffering is good." Look, hermit, how
The pavement aches and strains to be set free
And faces yearn to have their scars removed.
Go, let them suffer! Suffering is release. . .
Doctor of souls, empty of heart and mind, show us your peace!

"Only fi' cents
Buy a song"
Only fi' cents
Sing along

Hurry, hurry,
Let us be
Happy like
A rooted tree.

Sing and dance now,
Lover, shake
The fear out from me
Or I'll break—

Fear of lying
On the ground
Underneath
The feet that pound

Fear of whirling
With the wheel
Crushed between
The snapping steel

Fear of being
Without a bed
Asking strangers
For your bread.

"Only fi' cents
Buy a song"
Hurry lover,
Sing along—

5

Now travel east. Move down Carlton Street
Where narrow shadowed rooming houses clamp
The lid down tight on men and women; where
The cry of children is a rare phenomenon.
Barren the streets: people have overflowed
Into the Allan Gardens—green O green
Yellowed with bodies' sweat, ruffled with talk—
Until you plunge beyond the fountains and beyond
The newspapers grown musty on the ground
To Moss Park hovels, urchins in bare feet
And rags; a slouching shadow down a lane
And splintered floors to trap the feet of rats.

6

But there must be beauty somewheres, somewheres,
Kid yourself, keep telling yourself, Kid.
The steel-helmeted bird, relentless to Honolulu
Pilot spanning blue's outdistance,
They lie low together, loving. They know,
They speed in intimate connection
Pilot in plane, man in woman.
There is beauty somewheres
Not a hard street and a smashing hatred
Enemy shoulders brushing,
Not a fly teasing your face and gasoline in your nostrils.

But somewheres, somewheres
More than this blood branch of rowan berries
More than this wind heavy with hay-scent
Is the warm scent of the breath bent on a woman
Is beauty with connection caught
My fruit content in a warm womb.

7

It's good food for the birds, the old man said
Rifling a garbage can behind the Royal Bank.
His round eyes gleaming under a battered hat
He peered at dried out sandwiches, half-bitten crusts,
And nervous twitches cut across his mouth.
It's good food (where's the cop). Please lady, see
I'm such a benefactor, though I'm poor
(That can't be hid)—But see how kind I am!
Believe, believe! It's good food for the birds. . .

8

When I look at the Royal York
Shooting above hunger
Friendly with the sun, up there,
With its elevator heart pumping life
Pumping gold from cellar to summit—

When I look at the Royal York
Being interviewed by The Star
In an intimate, ingratiating way,
When I see the gold braced bell boy, the important clutch
Releasing service; and the dark chambermaid
Forever shaking snow-white sheets forever stained–

When I look at the Royal York
I am a shadow under a cold wall.

But when I look at man again
A thing scarce noticed by the sun, or mentioned in
The social columns; when I see
His legs, his overcoat, his hatless head
His hands held steady and his clearlit eyes—

Then I am tall as the Royal York,
For I built it!
The sun's distance is no chasm, for
I harnessed him with Copernicus
And Karl Marx, years ago!

Depression Suite

i

If there are prayers, it is the walls
That hear them, lavatory walls
And smart swift taps that spurt.

If there are tears, and cigarettes
It is the walls that hold such
And then erase the hurt.

If there are girls who still have left a song
The midnight scrubber does not heed
But mops it up like dirt.

This is the wall, the enemy
Who keeps our hands from striking free.

ii

I can be a vagabond and still
Be framed within a window sill;

I can nurse a little cloud
And yet not mention it aloud;

I can sing down deep within
And not let anybody in.

But I can't stretch a hand out yet
To someone I have never met

And shout the answer, stride the wall
Crying, here is room for all.

I am a coward yet, the task
Is too stupendous that you ask.

iii

I sit and hammer melodies
Upon the keys; the snappy tunes
Go pounding down the room; O quick
My girl! Yessir, and click click click,

She's at it harder still, the fear
Like rigid tentacles, like arms
Gripping her back; a wave of heat
Must be fought down, the lips drawn in

And faster faster, Sir, we have
Your letter of the fifteenth instant
How do you like my harmonies
Better than jazz dear Sir, click click.

Better than jazz and kisses are
The pounding minutes, nickels, dimes
The dancing whirling hours, the fear
The keys, quick, quick, the fear!

iv

You have no heart—
That's what she said:
You haven't a morsel
Of brains in your head.

You hobble along
Like a limping horse;
With face unshaven;
Your jokes are coarse.

You ask for a kiss
When I want a show:
Shall we go to a dance?
You reply, "Aw no."

It isn't any fun
Going with you
So don't come back.
That's all; I'm through.

❖ ❖ ❖ ❖

Well, I've been hungry
For a decent meal
Till the smell of coffee
Has made me reel.

I've had the soles
Of my shoes worn out
And shuffled in line
Like a turnabout.

The moon and the stars
Have lit the dark
As I slept on the ground
In a city park.

And morning has been
Raw white and chill
With an ache in the bones
And my mind stock still.

Yet there's a hunger
Worse than these:
When a girl goes by
Gay as you please

And a fellow meets her
And they smile deep—
That's a hunger
Won't let me sleep.

Makes me wonder
If I'm just
Like a lump
Of trodden dust

Sets me thinking
Faster yet;
Hurry, Mister
Don't forget

Thousands like us
Lying in bed—
"You have no heart"
The boss once said:

"You've only arms
And legs for me
Time in, time out—
And then you're free."

Free: to stumble
Down a street
With sullen look
And restless feet—

Thousands like us
Lying in bed:
We might be shouldering
Men, instead!

We might be marching
With firm tread—
"You have no heart"
That's what *she* said.

v

The boss was a friend of mine
I was close to his heart
(Snatch the plank from the saw)
Heave till your muscles smart)

The boss liked the way I ran
Fast as the mill hum
I, a revolving bee
And wood my honey comb.

Pile up, pile up for him
Sweet steaming logs that wheel
Blasted by logger's hands
Peeled raw by men and steel.

Speed up, speed up, the sweat
Greases our chains, our breath:
Never stumble nor pause
If a man is crushed to death.

The boss was a friend of mine—
I flashed my union card:
He spat and turned away
Slow, in the mill yard.

vi

The man you knew in Galilee
Walked also in the market-place,
Stood at the warrior's monument
With weather-beaten face.

Crying against the shrunken slums
He held the city Council mute—
Down in a Hastings Street café
He touched a prostitute.

He came back hungry from the camps,
Rattled a cup on bargain day
And selling flowers was sent to jail
For leading other men astray—

You who approve the Mountie's whip,
Tear gas, and the rearing beast:
Mark you the faces underfoot!
His was of these, the least.

Even although the skimpy relief investigator
Pressed by you in the hall, afraid of a hot glance
And you heard her thinking aloud: "Why don't they get jobs?"
      You're alive, still, alive!

Even although the woman you love is the one you can't marry—
You can fornicate and besmirch love, but never make it secure
(That's not allowed by the government)
      You are standing erect and alive

Even although Maisie looks furtively every day
At the bright dashing dress in the store window
And your hands seem pinned to your pockets

Even though fruit is spilled onto the sidewalk
Black thick grapes like a kid's curls, oranges,
Peaches like the sun going down, bananas

Even although you can't taste them
      You're alive, by yourself, alive.

You can smell the essence of sweet fall fruit
Summer itself falling and the sea wind changing
Clouds bluffing the sunlight

You can chase shadows and guffaw at prosperity's cower
You can stretch muscles and shout
You've got it, got what it takes
To be living, alive!

Dominion Day at Regina

We, from the prairies' sweep
reared with the wheatfields
who followed the gopher
home to his mating

Kin to the pine tree
tossed with sea foam
in rusty rock's heart
blasting a home

We from a mining town
seared with black dust
suckled on bosses' oath
schooled by our struggles

Give us no uniforms—
warm walls instead;
pierce with no bayonets
we ask for bread!

We offer our hands
our sinew and bone—
Give us the work
and it shall be done!

Comrade

Once only did I sleep with you;
And sleep and love again more sweet than I
Have ever known; without an aftertaste.
It was the first time; and a flower could not
Have been more softly opened, folded out.
Your hands were firm upon me: without fear
I lay arrested in a still delight—
Till suddenly the fountain in me woke.

My dear, it's years between; we've grown up fast
Each differently, each striving by itself.
I see you now a grey man without dreams,
Without a living, or an overcoat:
But sealed in struggle now, we are more close
Than if our bodies still were sealed in love.

I Never Hear

I never hear you are happy, nor
Whether wind spurs you, your clattering hoof-beats
Down the new road, the waving green.
I never hear, yet from my pillow
A laugh rockets through the dark:
Wind outside, tugging my muscles
Promises end of frost-bite—
Spring freshets, dancing hoofs.

Deep Cove: Vancouver

And still we dream, coiled in a mountain crevice
And still we let the sun
Shift on flesh and bone his subtle fingers
Before his day is run.

Comrade, the thrush will never give us warning:
His singing will not cease—
The bees will hum all down the darkest morning
Inveigling us to peace;

The mountains, yearning forward into silence
Have done with shaking; for the stir
Of centuries is only a brief wrinkle
Where the thunders were.

But we, who love to lie here hushed, immobile,
Whistling a low bird note
Can have no rest from clash of arms behind us
And thunder at the throat.

Here though we lie like lizards on a rock-ledge
Suckling the sun's breast—
Manhood and growth are on us; rise up, Comrade!
It is death to rest.

At English Bay: December, 1937

By the winter-stripped willows in the Park I walked
Gold-washed fountains in the sudden sun;
Brisk the air, white-capped the mountains,
Close at my feet the rim of the land's end—
Everything held in a silent axis, carved in sunlight
Except for the ocean pounding below me, relentless reminder:
Thoughts in my mind clear as heaven's azure
Till the heave, the roar of encroaching armies
Broke on my heart's shore.

Water that has washed the coasts of China,
Shanghai's city, yellow Yangtse;
Water that has cleansed the bloodied hands
And healed the wounds
Signed the death-warrant on too tell-tale lips
Sent to oblivion the iron ships;
Water forever restless, forever in struggle

As a man feels in himself his fevered spirit
Rising and falling, urging and being spent
Into new deeps and further continents—
Until he begins to move with others
Seizing the willows as banners—
Gold-washed fountains in the sudden sun!

Board Meeting: 1938

In the glass room
From rounded chairs sunk in the carpeted gloom
Cigar smoke and steam heat
My friends and colleagues rise on ponderous feet.
"To the King!" That's the thing.
The king is dead. Long live the king.

And wing of my heart, bird-note
Lie stifled in my throat.

And now we will hear the president's peroration
His eagle eye surveys the cares of nation
His altruistic pudgy fist
Pounds out the message words have missed.
To be followed by the vice-president
Back-seat driver
Who rains statistics on our heads—
And ends with the dividend, the umbrella.

Well modulated applause. Our hands too smooth
For smacking clap or iron-muscled putsch.
And now the moment of infinite regret
For deep respect, profound appreciation
(Here adjectives accrue like wealth
Gain interest in the deepest pocket):
"We are constrained to say farewell
To our oldest colleague
Our friend through thick and thin
Whom sickness has prevented..."

Bird wing, rise in my heart
Heart, rise to sheer walls, and beat
On glass and steel; break
Your way bleeding into homespun air.

Now I arise. To review the mass of years
This business put upon me; to say there was effort
(And not that it was vain); to cherish unity
(Wolf pack against the sheep); and honour words.
Now I arise, armed with certificates
To justify an honourable retirement
Sealed by the doctor, smiled on by the nurse—
Never to hint what every hawk's brain knows
What every tongue wags in the dark to wife:

That this one, treading to power with vigorous ease
Looked back— and saw the means to liquidation
The outstretched hunger parching in the sun:
This one in protest raised a hand, prepared
Himself an early funeral, death in the afternoon:
To which no mourners come, no toast is sung.

"My resignation, gentlemen. . ."

In the glass room
From rounded chairs sunk in the carpeted gloom
My friends and colleagues smoke cigars and stare.
The gavel falls:

> *A heart bursts into bloom,*
> *Crashes the upper air.*

Spain

When the bare branch responds to leaf and light
Remember them: it is for this they fight.
It is for haze-swept hills and the green thrust
Of pine, that they lie choked with battle dust.

You who hold beauty at your finger-tips
Hold it because the splintering gunshot rips
Between your comrades' eyes; hold it across
Their bodies' barricade of blood and loss.

You who live quietly in sunlit space
Reading The Herald after morning grace
Can count peace dear, when it has driven
Your sons to struggle for this grim, new heaven.

Catalonia

I

The flag of darkness lowers at half mast
Blotting the blood-stained hieroglyphs with eyes
Strained from the smoke, the flares, the rat-tat-tat
Of guns' incessant speech. A sudden lull
Fans wind on brow, betokens from far hills
The ones who rest—oh unbelievably
A girl who rests tired head on easy arm
And sleeps encircled by her own heart-beat.

But we, grey snakes who twist and squirm our way
From hump to sodden hump, roll in a hole
Of slime, scarring our knees to keep awake—
For us horizons reel, groping for a centre,
Stars burn in whirling sockets overhead—
We wrench ourselves over the last trench, down
Down, down in scurrying scramble tossed
Towards lost lines, lost outposts, lost defence. . .

2

The Captain of the Third Brigade
Sprang from a hillock where he peered
Into the flare-lit dark. He crouched
And doubled up, ran to the gunner's nest.

"They've quit" he hissed. "They've left the ridge—
Swarming to cover in the wood.
The tanks? They've left the bloody tanks
Defenceless. Wounded men will be inside."

Sorenson came up. He'd seen
The gashed retreat from our right flank.
Tall and lean as a stripped tree
He hung above the captain, panting words.

"What's that?" The Captain thrust a fist
In the man's face. "You mean it, Sorenson?"
"I'll go" the lean one said. And down
He slithered on his knees, towards the tanks.

3

Within a tank the smoky darkness stretched itself
And stupidly the air clutched at his face,
Acrid with oil. It shoved his nostrils in
Clung to his palate with a gritty clasp,
Burned in his lungs. He choked and coughed
Tried to restrict his chest from heaving rasps,
Crouched in his corner hard against the steel.
His ribs vibrated with each hammer stroke
Released in jerks from a machine-gun's maw.
Then he was hit. Fire stung his shoulder-blade
His arm, still bleeding, hung beside him limp—
A stranger's arm. He looked at it
And saw himself the same, inertly cut
From human contact, blood of brotherhood.
Then sweat broke on his brow, the blood closed down
Against all sound of guns. He swayed, and fell.

4

The boy he fell upon stirred in his dream
Moaned, and felt out the knife wound in his side.
The soggy bandages were now a wad of blood
Clotted but unavailing. Pain
Throbbed like a heartbeat pounding through the room
—His room at home he thought, all sheltered in
With slanting shafts of light, the chinks of day
Touching this rosy plastered wall, with chairs

Hunch-backed, the cool tile floors with candle grease
Spattered like silver coins beside the bed. . .
But oh, the voice—what voice sang out to him
Screaming in siren tones, arise, awake
Stand up and strike, strike, fight and shoot
Shoot till the last strip fumbles in your hand
And silence yawns about you in the tank.

The tank! He rose up on one arm
Then crawled away from his companion's side.
The fumes, the oily fumes spluttered within his brain.
He dragged himself upright and at the hole
Peered out upon the heaving earth, where still
The blasted flowers of fire bloomed high.

The boy was yet alive, upright, awake
When Sorenson burst open the tank door
And hauled him out. "Here's bandages and here
This rifle you can lean upon and walk"—
The other one was dead. They took his gun
And letters spilling from his pockets, these
The two remembered; then ploughed on to find
The next tank, and the next, where other men
Lay trapped and helpless, ammunition gone.

Now we retreat in better order, confident
Of gun on shoulder, captain in command
The wounded swing in swift-made hammocks, safe
From a long guttering death within a tank.

People are marching down the roads of Spain
Bundled with babies, chattels, straggling tots
A donkey-load of warmth, a basket, light
With bits of bread, dried beans, remains
Of other hasty meals swallowed between
The zoom of air raids over village streets.
People are marching with all song
Gone out, all sunlight flattened grey
Upon their faces. Now in steady haste
Marching to valleys where the mountain shade
Leans kindly down, where snow
Looks fair to sleep upon. No winds can blow
More fiercely than a bomb, the winter's cold
Will be steel needles, lighter far to bear
Than thrust of shrapnel splitting through the skin.
People are marching, marching, and they meet
The tattered tunics of the soldiers, some of whom
Walk bareback in the cold. The people stop
And give a shawl, a skirt for covering
And men march on ahead. March on to make
A further stand.

        Though darkness fall again,
A tattered flag, the men will stand upright,
Spirit sustained, the floor of Spain
A ground not tilled in vain with blood
With bones of young men scattered far;
Not fertilized in vain, O grey-green gloss
Of olives, wind-bent on a hill, of earth
Supported by the vineyards' yield, and wheat
Crisp in the sun. No more sterility
Or drouth or barrenness is yours
O rolling plains: who make a covering now
For breath and bone; for growing hands
Whose fingers work between the roots, to burst
Out of the earth again, another spring!

Words before Battle

When, in a Moscow hospital
You cried: "Abyssinia!" Barbusse,
And died—we few remembered.

The hot molten liquid
Of words poured out in hope
And defeat—these have burned us.

Now in self scrutiny,
Remembering your friend in song,
Lorca, shot like a dog—

Remembering thin tunics in Spain
Words riddled from the mouths
Of men by man-made steel,

Remembering the Czechs beaten
To their knees without
A fight, gagged by the wayside:

Now we know our strength
Has been as the strength of one,
Our will as water, our words

Not bitter shafts of light
Striking the people; echoes
Only, of words to be said.

Now, precipitate
In darkness, we have found
Your cry unmemorized.

Energy has been spilled
On the floor, not conserved
In a glass jar for winter,

Struggle has been blind,
Relying too much on the fist
Bared to the teeth of guns.

It is not enough to be proud
And sure, shouting defiance;
It is not enough to ignore

The enemy's cunning, his sheer
Weight of steel, his mountains
Of iron and chromium

His breastplates gleaming
His bombers diving
His metal raining, driving—

It is not enough to foreshorten
Time's movement, to say:
"Tomorrow will be the day."

It was not enough for you,
Barbusse, nor for those slain
About Thermopylae.

And in this ominous
Barbed peace, we know:
It is not enough for us.

Autumn: 1939

In our time the great ones fade
We hear the whisper of their falling
Words on a radio announce
How Yeats and Freud within a year
Heard the insistent silence calling.

In our time torpedoes score
In thunder-foam the ships go under
Blood is spurted from the sky
Ashes smoke where children played—
Gardens, pavements, split in plunder.

In our time no great ones live
For ears are censored from their singing—
No surgeon of the mind can touch
Pillar of salt, idiot stare,
Bell-tongues meaninglessly swinging.

The Lizard: October, 1939

No one has come from the fronts we knew—
Shanghai and Yenan— for a long session:
Silent now the Madrid broadcasts. So was Vienna once
Blotted out. We remember her voices fading.
No one has come. Letters unanswered. The stricken
Refugees smothered then, after
Years of ditch stumbling?
The battling, thin tunics gored to death
In the country of the bull, in the country of the dragon?

In the sheltered rocks of our homeland, the Pacific waters
Hills shrouded with evergreen and the valleys yellow
With corn and apples; within the walls of our houses
Splashed with a vivid wallpaper,
Radios blare the censored version of our living:
Wrestlers rage, baseball bouncers rant,
The words of a recipe tinkle on the ear—
Lord Halifax speaks sprightly from London
Where the people run about gladly
Attending to air-raid precautions.

In the sheltered rocks, stealthily, a lizard
Slips hesitant into sunlight; tunes himself
To the wind's message. We slip out in pairs, as lovers
Strip ourselves, longing
To see bodies bare and flesh uncloseted,
To hear real voices again, to uphold the song
Of one coming from Madrid, Shanghai or Yenan
Bearers of good news
From the fronts we knew.

Speak through Me

Speak through me, mountains.
Your granite wisdom, the walled heart of your patience,
Arrest me.
Mention the small life quivering in your armpits
Moss, lichen and the blue rock flowers;
Speak of the pheasant running to cover
And the grouse drums calling.
Draw me to the bare high ribs
Where the sun takes his pleasure
Urge me to the rare coolness of your brow
Where the snow's light dazzles—
Bewilder me with your height and your gaze to seaward
Shock my senses with your vibrant stillness.

Speak through me, mountains
Till the other voices be silent
Till the sirens cease and the guns muffle their thunder
Till the monstrous voice of man is sheltered by quiet—
Speak through me, speak till I remember
Movement in the womb and green renewal
Sundrenched maples in September
And the sweep of time as a gull's wing slanting.

From Day And Night
(1939-1944)

Seven Poems
for Duncan

i

A shell burst in my mind
Upheaving roots since birth, perhaps, confined
Before I dreamed
The devastation there outlined.

And so my body now
Owes no allegiance to the scythe and plough:
I, dispossessed
Count no blossoms on the bough.

I build on no man's land
A city not my own, with others planned
By others dreamed,
And with a new race forged and manned!

ii

From the husk of the old world
To the new I fly
Strong winds beating
In a bluer sky

Where old men stretch not
Their vampire necks
And young men vaunt not
Their sunburnt backs

Where jewelled women
With glittering breasts
Suck not the life-blood
From young nests

But where the cradled
Infant rocks
While cloudy sheep
Caress his locks

And where the golden
Apples blow
In easy bliss
Upon a bough

iii

Out of the turmoil mustered by day
We may not free our hands, nor turn our heads to pray—
So tight the knot our sunlight ties.

So firm the hold of voices, thoughts are drowned
The river's chant is lost, in splintering gunshot sound:
Or from its song the essence dies.

Brightness was all, when earth lay primitive
Fair to the hands' fresh touch, ready to burst and live:
Now in her womb corrosion lies.

Therefore we search alone the shuttered dark
Where faces of the dead shine luminous, a spark
Of lightning from encircled skies:

Therefore we seek the peace of broken ground
After the wars have buried all the young, and found
Dark remedy for shining eyes. . .

Therefore we hide our faces; make no sound.

iv

On a night like this, the Ides of March perhaps,
Spring will arrest your muscles and a raid
Of hands will light on you, and cry out: "Choose."
Incisive fingers on your shoulder-blade,
Open sockets for stampeding news.

"Listen child." And you know the answer held
You face the pitiless eyes and open wide
Your own, like shock observers; as they say
The words no fluttering flag of fear could hide:
"The operation failed. He died today."

And if the words were different: "War's declared."
There is no difference, the thought is one.
This the expected shock, the Judas-kiss
A flower cup uncurling into sun
Childhood's leaves warned by the dark of this.

We grew, and munitions matched us, laboratories
Weighed the ingredients; magnifying glass
Revealed death's desert in a finger-nail
Of dust. Whatever door we sought to pass
Was marked with chalk. All sesames would fail.

This is not news, but a resolution passed
After hard labour, bitterness of sides.
Tenseness relaxed, you knew it all your days:
There would be one man missing, one who hides
His cunning hand from thunder with the "nays."

Impartially the chairman-undertaker
Smiling casts his vote, announces death
Speculates on population where
Our wombs are lacerated, lovers' breath
Is torn asunder in the cool March air.

We are the children long prepared for dust
Ready in bone, the wrist a pulsing pain:
On a precarious railway-rib we lie
Our limbs long ready for the armoured train—
Ears to the ground and bare eyes to the sky.

v

The fallow mind in winter knows, its scope
And wide horizon are made narrow by
The rim of early dusk, descending blinds—
Last summer's rocket buried under sand.
To soar and spin, to take the hand and whip
A leash of fiery comets through the sky:
To be crier or prophet, John or Isaiah, these
Wait in the mind for the world's turning phase:
The time she lifts her head from blood-soaked fields,
From one-eyed houses, shattered, gaping towns,
The time she sees her brother sun, and bares
Her ribs to his remembered healing blaze—
Then will the mind take a new stature on
And children thrive, who late last year were bombed.

vi

The child looks out from doors too high and wide for him
On words spun large as suns, huge meanings sprayed on
    tree
And roadway, spreading fields, not to be caught and
    clapped
Together in a rosy nave, the sun no coin
For fingers to indent.   The child runs out to stare
At masterful young men who bat a tennis ball
At giants in kilt skirts whose march is purposeful
At mothers in cool gowns who move about like moons
Upon the eternal lawns, low laughter shimmering
About their curving mouths.   The child leans on the future,
Slender tree ungainly rooted there by private worlds
Who knew a private ecstasy unshared by him
But let the memory slip and reared a hedge
Of bristling phrases, last year's bills, and week-ends
    snatched
In secret hate; his room laid waste when radios
Are tuned, when rumour's blatant voice hits nerve,
Dries tissue, brittles down
The new unmoulded bone.

                              The child in cities toddling up
A stifling reach of stair, gains window-seat:
How consternation puckers up his eyes—at space
Unplanted, seed unwanted, wars unwarranted
Consuming his small, thankless growing place!

                    vii

And life goes on. And here
We hold a leaf upon the eyes
And its green ribs press down like veins
Into the nerve and sinew of ourselves.
Your finger-tip on eyelid, or my brows
Bent in the conclave of your cheek,
Spur vibrant nerve to life, adhere like leaf to stem
Stem into tree, tree rooted into earth.

No hazard here, for we
Like sleepers plunging deep
Into recurring waves of dream
Cannot awake from that connected bliss.
We are asleep on the long limb of time.

The Outrider
Swift outrider of lumbering earth.
                    — C. Day Lewis
for Raymond Knister

PROLOGUE

He who was alien has retraced the road
Unleashed, returns to this familiar earth.
The gate falls open at his touch, the house
Receives him without wonder, as an elm
Accepts her brood of birds. Along his road
Crows charivari chattering announce
His coming to each thronging sentry-post.

The old man standing with his hayfork high
Can let it rest, mid-air, and burden fails
And falls within the sun-dipped gloom of barn.
The young boy bowed behind the clicking mow
Feels his spine stiffen as if birds had whirred
Behind him, or a storm had clapped its clouds.
A girl, chin pressed upon a broom, will stir
As a warm wave of wonder sweeps her out
Whither her musings never leapt before.
And so it is.

        His coming dreamed of long
In the recesses of thinking, in the hard
Hills climbed, his face a resting-place.
In winter warming hands at roaring stove
His doings crackling as autumn wood. . .
And so it is. Now summer's all swept clean
He comes with eyes more piercing than before
And scrapes his boots—swinging wide the door.

I

The year we came, it was all stone picking:
Sun on your fiery back, and the earth
Grimly hanging on to her own. At the farm's end
A cedar bog to clear. But in the dry season
Not enough drink for the cattle.
The children gathered blueberries, and ate corn meal.
We danced no festivals.

Children stretched lean to manhood. One day
Wind prying round, wrenched free the barn
And lightning had the whole hay crop
Flaming to heaven. Trying to save the horse
Arthur was stifled. His black bones
We buried under the elm.

I stumble around now, trying to see it clearly.
Incessantly driven to feed our own ones, but friendly
        to neighbours:
Not like the crows, hungry for goslings,
But sober, sitting down Sunday for rest-time
Contented with laughter.

I stumble around now, lame old farm dog:
When I'm gone, one less hunger
And the hay still to be mown.

The buggy on that whirling autumn day
Swayed in a rain rut, nearly overturned.
And you stood by the roadside, brown and gay,
Black hair drawn tight in pigtails and your eyes
Searching the sky. Brave was your body then
And I brought you home to discover the answer to
        hunger,
The peace of loving, the stay of restlessness.

Trembling as a birch tree to a boy's swinging
You were again and again my own small love.
But love was never enough, though children sprang
Year after year from your loins—never enough
For my yearning though your eyes burned strangely—
And earth has kept you far more fierce and safe.

My mother caught me in her skirts and tossed me high
        high into hay I bounced.
The straw tickled and a swallow, frightened, flew
        before my heart could cry.

I remember this, the startling day of early fear,
        bird beating me back
And somehow no way—hard to know why or where
        she was no longer near.

Brothers would later tease me with a feather tail
        or loose a crow they caught
And I must swallow the fear with my hunger, to learn
        how the yearned for will fail

How the expected sunlight will shrivel your pounding heart,
        the seed you plant be killed
The apple be bitter with worm, but your honesty firm
        seeking another start.

I grew up one evening, much alone—
Resolved to plunge. The thing I feared, the crow,
Was hoarse with calling, whirling, diving down
And suddenly his urgent social bent
Was answer to my inwardness. His cry
Throbbed and echoed in my head, his wings
Caught all reflections in my mirrored mind.
I would then follow where his footless tread
Led on; I would no longer be the beast
Who ploughed a straight line to the barrier
And swung back on his steps—my father's son.
It would take long. But from that summer on
My heart was set. I raced through swinging air,
Rumpled my head with laughter in the clouds.

2

It was different, different
From the thoughts I had.
Asphalt and factory walls are not
Soft ending to a road.

It was different, different
Standing tight in line
Forgetting buffeting clouds above
Trying to look a man.

It was different, different
To lift the lever arm
And see farm beasts revolving by
Their dripping blood still warm.

On lazier afternoons
Deep in clover scent
Neither beast nor I could dream
What the speed-up meant.

A thousand men go home
And I a thousandth part
Wedged in a work more sinister
Than hitching horse and cart.

Dark because you're beaten
By a boss's mind:
A single move uneven turned
Will set you in the wind.

His mercy is a calculation
Worse than a hurricane—
Weather you can grumble at
But men can make you groan.

(Down in the washroom
    leaflets are passed.
"Say, Joe, you sure
    got those out fast."

"Yes. Now's the time
    to give them the gate:
Speed-up right here
    is legitimate!"

An old worker stares:
    his wizened face
Sceptical still—
    Years in the trace.

But young, lean face
    opposite me
Reads, and alert
    watches to see

Who will respond
    who's first to talk—
Our eyes meet, and greet
    as a key fits a lock.)

Early morning
stirs the street
men go by
on urgent feet.

Early morning
litter still
in the gutters
on the sill.

Early morning
sky shows blue
men are marching
two and two.

Men are surging
past the gate
where last week no one
dared be late:

Surging—though
a siren's shrieks
warn that someone
called the dicks. . .

It was different, different
Because I learned: for this
You plough the fields and scatter
The toil of days and years.

You die in harness and are proud
Of earthen servitude
While others that live in chains have sought
To shake the rotting wood

Upheave the very earth, if need
Insist, banish the fence
Between a neighbour's grudging hate
Rise in your own defence

Against the smooth-tongued salesman
"The cottage built for two"
The haggling on market days
Desperate to know

How winter's service shall be slaved—
Will this hay last the year—
Where are the taxes coming from—
Must we sell the mare?

Cities that sell their toil, must put
Possessiveness to shame
And draw you to them in the fight:
The battle is the same.

The blowing silver barley grain
And skyline wide, serene—
These shall be your gift to those
Who wield the world's machine!

This is your signpost: follow your hands, and dig.
After, the many will have parachutes
For air delight. Not veering with the crow
But throbbing, conscious, knowing where to go.
There's time for flying. Dig up crumbling roots,
Eradicate the underbrush and twig—
Pull snapping thistle out and stubborn sloe—
Those backward ramblers who insist they know.

Employ your summertime, at union rate:
Conveying energy on this green belt
Of earth assembled, swiftly known and felt.
Faster! Speed-up is here legitimate:
Employ your summertime, before the thrust
Of winter wind would harden down the dust.

EPILOGUE

We prayed for miracles: the prairie dry,
Our bread became a blister in the sun;
We watched the serene untouchable vault of sky
—In vain our bitter labour had been done.

We prayed to see the racing clouds at bay
Rumpled like sheets after a night of joy,
To stand quite still and let the deluged day
Of rain's releasing, surge up and destroy.

We prayed for miracles, and had no wands
Nor wits about us; strained in a pointed prayer
We were so many windmills without hands
To whirl and drag the water up to air.

A runner sent ahead, returned with news:
"There is no milk nor honey flowing there.
Others allay the thirst with their own blood
Cool with their sweat, and fertilize despair."

O new found land! Sudden release of lungs,
Our own breath blows the world! Our veins, unbound
Set free the fighting heart. We speak with tongues—
This struggle is our miracle new found.

Day and Night

1

Dawn, red and angry, whistles loud and sends
A geysered shaft of steam searching the air.
Scream after scream announces that the churn
Of life must move, the giant arm command.
Men in a stream, a moving human belt
Move into sockets, every one a bolt.
The fun begins, a humming, whirring drum—
Men do a dance in time to the machines.

2

One step forward
Two steps back
Shove the lever,
Push it back

While Arnot whirls
A roundabout
And Geoghan shuffles
Bolts about.

One step forward
Hear it crack
Smashing rhythm—
Two steps back

Your heart-beat pounds
Against your throat
The roaring voices
Drown your shout

Across the way
A writhing whack
Sets you spinning
Two steps back—

One step forward
Two steps back.

3

Day and night are rising and falling
Night and day shift gears and slip rattling
Down the runway, shot into storerooms
Where only arms and a note-book remember
The record of evil, the sum of commitments.
We move as through sleep's revolving memories
Piling up hatred, stealing the remnants,
Doors forever folding before us—
And where is the recompense, on what agenda
Will you set love down? Who knows of peace?

Day and night
Night and day
Light rips into ribbons
What we say.

I called to love
Deep in dream:
Be with me in the daylight
As in gloom.

Be with me in the pounding
In the knives against my back
Set your voice resounding
Above the steel's whip crack.

High and sweet
Sweet and high
Hold, hold up the sunlight
In the sky!

Day and night
Night and day
Tear up all the silence
Find the words I could not say. . .

4

We were stoking coal in the furnaces; red hot
They gleamed, burning our skins away, his and mine.
We were working together, night and day, and knew
Each other's stroke; and without words, exchanged
An understanding about kids at home,
The landlord's jaw, wage-cuts and overtime.
We were like buddies, see? Until they said
That nigger is too smart the way he smiles
And sauces back the foreman; he might say
Too much one day, to others changing shifts.
Therefore they cut him down, who flowered at night
And raised me up, day hanging over night—
So furnaces could still consume our withered skin.

Shadrach, Meshach and Abednego
Turn in the furnace, whirling slow.
    Lord, I'm burnin' in the fire
    Lord, I'm steppin' on the coals
    Lord, I'm blacker than my brother
    Blow your breath down here.

    Boss, I'm smothered in the darkness
    Boss, I'm shrivellin' in the flames
    Boss, I'm blacker than my brother
    Blow your breath down here.
Shadrach, Meshach and Abednego
Burn in the furnace, whirling slow.

5

Up in the roller room, men swing steel
Swing it, zoom; and cut it, crash.
Up in the dark the welder's torch
Makes sparks fly like lightning reel.

Now I remember storm on a field
The trees bow tense before the blow
Even the jittering sparrows' talk
Ripples into the still tree shield.

We are in storm that has no cease
No lull before, no after time
When green with rain the grasses grow
And air is sweet with fresh increase.

We bear the burden home to bed
The furnace glows within our hearts:
Our bodies hammered through the night
Are welded into bitter bread.

Bitter, yes:
But listen, friend:
We are mightier
In the end.

We have ears
Alert to seize
A weakness
In the foreman's ease

We have eyes
To look across
The bosses' profit
At our loss.

Are you waiting?
Wait with us
After evening
There's a hush—

Use it not
For love's slow count:
Add up hate
And let it mount

Until the lifeline
Of your hand
Is calloused with
A fiery brand!

Add up hunger,
Labour's ache
These are figures
That will make

The page grow crazy
Wheels go still,
Silence sprawling
On the till—

Add your hunger,
Brawn and bones,
Take your earnings:
Bread, not stones!

6

Into thy maw I commend my body
But the soul shines without
A child's hands as a leaf are tender
And draw the poison out.

Green of new leaf shall deck my spirit
Laughter's roots will spread:
Though I am overalled and silent
Boss, I'm far from dead!

One step forward
Two steps back
Will soon be over:
Hear it crack!

The wheels may whirr
A roundabout
And neighbour's shuffle
Drown your shout

The wheel must limp
Till it hangs still
And crumpled men
Pour down the hill.

Day and night
Night and day
Till life is turned
The other way!

Lorca
for Federico Garcia Lorca,
Spanish poet, shot, it was said, by Franco's men

When veins congeal
And gesture is confounded
When pucker frowns no more
And voice's door
Is shut forever

On such a night
My bed will shrink
To single size
Sheets go cold
The heart hammer
With life-loud clamour
While someone covers up the eyes.

Ears are given
To hear the silence driven in
Nailed down.
And we descend now down from heaven
Into earth's mould, down.

While you—
You hold the light
Unbroken.

When you lived
Day shone from your face:
Now the sun rays search
And find no answering torch.

If you were living now
This cliffside tree
And its embracing bough
Would speak to me.

If you were speaking now
The waves below
Would be the organ stops
For breath to blow.

And if your rigid head
Flung back its hair
Gulls in a sickle flight
Would circle there.

> *You make the flight
> Unshaken.*

You are alive!
O grass flash emerald sight
Dash of dog for ball
And skipping rope's bright blink
Lashing the light!

High in cloud
The sunset fruits are basketed
And fountains curl their plumes
On statue stone.
In secret thicket mould
Lovers defend their hold,
Old couples hearing whisperings
Touch in a handclasp, quivering.

For you sang out aloud
Arching the silent wood
To stretch itself, tiptoe,
Above the crowd...

> *You hold the word*
> *Unspoken.*

You breathe. You be.
Bare, stripped light
Time's fragment flagged
Against the dark.

You dance. Explode
Unchallenged through the door
As bullets burst
Long deaths ago, your heart.

And song outsoars
The bomber's range
Serene with wind-
Manoeuvred cloud.

> *Light flight and word*
> *The unassailed, the token!*

Prelude for Spring

These dreams abound:
Foot's leap to shore
Above the sound
Of river's roar—
Disabled door
Banged and barricaded.
Then on, on
Furrow, fawn
Through wall and wood
So fast no daring could
Tear off the hood
Unmask the soul pursued.

Slash underbrush
Tear bough and branch
Seek cover, rabbits' burrow—
Hush!

He comes. Insistent, sure
Proud prowler, this pursuer comes
Noiseless, no wind-stir
No leaf-turn over;
Together quiet creeps on twig,
Hush hovers in his hands.

How loud heart's thump—
Persistent pump
Sucks down, down sap
Then up in surge
(Axe striking stump).

How breezy breath—
Too strong a wind
Scatters a stir
Where feathers are,
Bustles a bough.

How blind two eyes
Shuttling to-fro
Not weaving light
Nor sight. . .
In darkness flow.

(Only the self is loud;
World's whisperless.)

Dive down then, scuttle under:
Run, fearless of feet's thunder.
Somehow, the road rolls back in mist
Here is the meadow where we kissed
And here the horses, galloping
We rode upon in spring. . .

O beat of air, wing beat
Scatter of rain, sleet,
Resisting leaves,
Retarding feet

And drip of rain, leaf drip
Sting on cheek and lip
Tearing pores
With lash of whip

And hoof's away, heart's hoof
Down greening lanes, with roof
Of cherry blow
And appie puff—

O green wet, sun lit
Soaked earth's glitter!
Down mouth, to munch
Up hoof, to canter

Through willow lanes
A gold-shaft shower,
Embracing elms
That lack leaf-lustre

And copse' cool bed
All lavendered
With scentless, sweet
Hepatica—

Till side by side
In fields' brown furrow
Swathe sunlight over
Every shadow!

But still
On heart's high hill
And summit of
A day's delight

Still will he swoop
From heaven's height
Soaring unspent,
Still will he stoop to brush
Wing tip on hair,
Fan mind with fear.

And now the chill
Raw sun
Goes greener still—
The sky
Cracks like an icicle:

Frozen, foot-locked
Heart choked and chafed
Wing-battered and unsafe,
Grovel to ground!
A cry
Lashes the sky—

These dreams abound.

Serenade for Strings

for Peter

i

At nine from behind the door
The tap tapping
Is furtive, insistent:
Recurrent, imperative
The I AM crying
Exhorting, compelling.

At eleven louder!
Wilderness shaking
Boulders uprolling
Mountains creating

And deep in the cavern
No longer the hammer
Faintly insistent
No longer the pickaxe
Desperate to save us
But minute by minute
The terrible knocking
God at the threshold!
Knocking down darkness
Battering daylight.

ii

O green field
O sun soaked
On lavish emerald
Blade and sharp bud piercing
O green field
Cover and possess me
Shield me in brightness now
From the knocking
The terrible knocking. . . .

iii

Again. . . Again. . . O again.
Midnight. A new day.
Day of days
Night of nights
Lord of lords.

Good Lord deliver us
Deliver us of the new lord
Too proud for prison
Too urgent for the grave. . .
Deliver us, deliver us.

> *O God the knocking*
> *The knocking attacking*
> *No breath to fight it*
> *No thought to bridge it*
> *Bare body wracked and writhing*
> *Hammered and hollowed*
> *To airless heaving.*

iv

The clock now. Morning.
Morning come creeping
Scrublady slishing
And sloshing the waxway
And crying O world
Come clean
Clean for the newborn
The sun soon rising. . .

Rising and soaring
On into high gear...
Sudden knowledge!
Easy speedway
Open country
Hills low-flying
Birds up-brooding
Clouds caressing
A burning noon-day...

Now double wing-beat
Breasting body
Till cloudways open
Heaven trembles:
   And blinding
     searing
       terrifying
        cry!

The final bolt has fallen.
The firmament is riven.

v

Now it is done.
Relax. Release.
And here, behold your handiwork:
Behold—a man!

Five Poems
for Marcia

i

In the dream was no kiss
No banners were upshaken
The sure, unsevered bonds of bliss
Were the hands untaken

In the dream no faltering
Grew between your tree and mine
Wind silenced us and sun embraced
We seized no outward sign

In the dream all burden fell
Sheer away; bare breathing left—
Bare eyes and light-cleft minds were formed
And found, never to be bereft.

It was the dream I saw again
Meeting your person in the room
The dream, electrified. Since, I am free:
Bird funnelling night flight alone.

ii

Your face is new; strange;
Yet infinitely known
Loved in some century
Grass swept, tree sown.

I memorize
The lineaments, so lean
Steel bird prey intent
Flight imminent

I see your stride (no walk)
Cleaving the air,
Cloud treading, your hair
Sickle bent.

O early, early
Before dawn whispers
Before day fingers
The faulty doorway

Early in the late
Moon-tossed night
Your face a flash
Foreruns the light.

iii

Early I lifted the oars of day
Sped over silent water
Early the wings of gulls found shadow
Sky's face flashing, mirrored.

Early morning is heart alone
No man shouting, no one
No planes soaring, death destroying
No shattered street a ruin.

Early is barely reachable
Soars beyond our knowing:
We are late sleepers, drugged in dark
Aliens all, to morning. . .

iv

Night's soft armour welds me into thought
Pliant and all engaging; warm dark,
No scintillations to distract
Nor any restless ray, moon-shot.
I am still of all but breathing—
No throbbing eye, no pulse; and a hushed heart.

Sometimes at rest, the bones assume
World's weight, hold us dumb
We cannot lift a finger, flick
An eyelash, wag a tongue:
Breath is only the fluctuation in
Death's posture, stony, dumb.

Then is all sound fled
Flown from the fluted ear
Wind in the heavy head
Can find no corridor

And then is sight so bound
Lids petrified to earth
Only one light is found—
Imagination's going forth!

Only the heaven sent
Pulse of the universe
Beats through the buried heart
Its steady course.

v

Your words beat out in space—
Distant drums under the hum of day
Only the hunter hurries for
Only the parched heart hears.

Look, it takes long to grow a listener
To bend his bough, let fall his leaf to earth;
Upward and on his own words speeding
Leaps the self to light.

But wind is teacher. Rain is kind
Down-sailing, soaking deep
And summer ruddying to sere
Reiterates the drift:

Be earthward bound; and here
In the strata of flown flowers
And skeleton of leaf, set self down
Hurry ear to ground.

Not burials; not dust and ashes' crumbs
But world's own cry resounding!
The spacious, the distant, army of your answer
The fast approaching drums.

Fantasia
for Helena Coleman, Toronto poet

And I have learned how diving's done
How breathing air, cool wafted trees
Clouds massed above the man-made tower
How these
Can live no more in eye and ear:
And mind be dumb
To all save Undine and her comb.

Imagination's underworld: where child goes down
Light as a feather. Water pressure
Hardly holds him, diving's easy
As the flight of bird in air
Or bomber drumming to his lair.

Child goes down, and laughingly
(He's not wanted yet, you see)
Catches fishes in his hand
Burrows toe in sifting sand
Seizes all the weeds about
To make a small sub-rosa boat

Then up he bobs, as easily
As any blown balloon
To greet the bosky, brooding sky
And hunger for the sun.

And child grown taller, clothed in man's
Long limbs, and shaggy hair, his chin outthrust
Searches for years the rounded world
Climbs to its peaks, falls to its valleys green
Striding the trim and trailing towns
Fingering the fond arteries
Possessing things, and casting them
Cloakwise to earth for sleeping time...

Sometime the lust wanderer
Will sleep, will pause; will dream of plunging deep
Below it all, where he will need
No clock companion, thorn in flesh, no contact man
To urge him from the ground.
For flying's easy, if you do it diving
And diving is the self unmoored
Ranging and roving—man alone.

And I have learned how diving's done
Wherefore the many, many
Chose the watery stair
Down, down Virginia
With your fêted hair
Following after Shelley
Or wordcarvers I knew
(Bouchette; and Raymond, you)—
Here is the fascination
Of the salty stare:
And death is here.
Death courteous and calm, glass-smooth
His argument so suave, so water-worn
A weighted stone.

And death's deliberation, his
Most certain waiting-room
His patience with the patient, who will be
His for infinity...

So no astounded peerers
On the surface craft
No dragging nets, no cranes
No gnarled and toughened rope
Not any prayer nor pulley man-devised
Will shake the undersea
Or be
More than a brief torpedo, children's arrow
More than a gaudy top outspun
Its schedule done...

Wise to have learned: how diving's done
How breathing air, cool wafted trees
Clouds massed above the man-made tower
How these
Can live no more in eye and ear:
And mind be dumb
To all save Undine and her comb...

West Coast: 1943
for Earle Birney

PRELUDE

This hour: and we have seen a shabby town change face,
the sandy soil be stripped of evergreen
and broom, born yellow into golden May
scrapped farther up Grouse Mountain. We, who lay
in roses and green shade under the cherry tree
we too were rooted up, set loose to beg
or borrow a new roof, accept a poorer view.
The tide had turned. That early gull adrift
on empty inlet, keel to sun, he was outrun
by humming plane, the flying boat on trial;
and pleasure schooner skirting the dark shore
was soon forced into harbour; for the grey gaunt giants,
hunters of skyline, convoy cruisers, they
jostled the bay.

        We saw the shoreline ripped
and boxes set in tidy rows, a habitation for
a thousand children swept from farm and mine
drawn to the hungry suction of the sea;
and saw the sunny slip where ferries sauntered in
easing their stragglers into a sleepy street
suddenly ablaze! And walls reared up, ship high,
grim curtain for machine-gun rat-tat-tat
as caulkers set to work and welders steered
the starry shrapnel on a new-laid keel.
Where two or three had come, travellers to be met
or mountain hikers holidaying high,
now in a herd of thundering hard heels
men surged for shop and ways, ten thousand strong
and bent for business, eager to belong.

High on our hill we watched, and knew
morning become high noon, and the tide full.

He who knew heaven is coming down the mountain
is stirred with wonder; curious, even he,
who bent eyes bookward in his earliest days
sucking the sunlight from a world of words
dreaming to be word-welder, builder of these.
Then up, and thoughts away, and books stamped under
up to the gravelled trail, the crags far yonder
where sun and rain blazed bliss on him
night chasing day on snow-spilt mountain rim.
He who knew heaven stands among us, watching
his hand unfitted to this hammer-hold,
his heart not conscious of the anvil-beat,
no visor for his eyes. Now he
makes ships? For carrying love in hold,
for salting down old wisdom into kegs
for other hands to welcome—yes and yes!
But ships for men to fight upon,
ships to right the wrong upon?—
He hardly knows; he hesitates.

And all about men flatten out the steel
with hammer beat, beat hammer, hammer beat,
shape it with sweat and muscle, shaped to fit
the muzzle of a ship, a new sea-bird.
And all about the masked men strike the torch
shaping the sides of ships with plate on plate
riveting bolts with sea-resistant spark.
From ship to ship, galley to hold, the pattern-makers move
until a new keel's laid, another scaffolding;
till fire and sweat, muscle and oath and jest
mingle to launch her down the vaulted ways—
a pearl-grey pointer leashed against the quays.

And why? What heaven-sent wanderer
could see the anthill swarm, and be at ease?
Could carry a load of tools or wheel a truck
to sling steel rods onto a derrick train?
He watched a day or so; waited his time
stood in the blacksmith's doorway where the furnaces
bellied and glared, vomiting molten steel
till the great moulder caught and shouldered it,
machine's male hands on feminine soft flesh
creating features, fittings for a bride—
a child of ocean still at berth, unscarred.

Challenged, mind moved, but not to the blood warmed
excitement seething in nerves' crevices
the ship, he saw, a symbol of conception
a giant scheme rearing to sky fruition.
But yet he stood without; a stranger still,
one hesitant to knock.

On morning shift, when sky and water melt
when men and women pour, with swinging pails
from ferry slip
pass through the gates, are billeted
and move, alert, toward the long grey shape
to find their home, their roof—
on morning shift, song burst from below the decks.
True as a bell, along the dock rang
Andalusian love song; high amidships
rumble of the rumba; in the hold
a youngster jived; and girls at hand
trousered and kerchiefed, busy hammering,
whistled clear the call to Coolins.
Song! Song from the throat of morning bursting
high above rivet, chipper, torch—
song from the hearts of men at labour
welding their words into the ship's side.

I

Who have from mountain wall
tunnelled to dark pits
where gas reeks, where weak light is life;
who have on mountain side,
meagre as table bare, taken a wife
made children, reared a roof;
who fought in strikes and met starvation
then back to pits again to face damnation
the dust sticking in throat, the cough, collapse.
Then from the Sanitarium, down to sea
to sea-coast air where men were building ships—
who breathe now, who find voice
and sing with the throat bare.

Who have through hail and storm, through endless rain
cherished the crop, husbanded our flock.
Have builded fences, reared high dykes
shifted the barn to upper ground
and with the hay half harvested, seen cloud
crouch low again to pelt destruction down:
seen trees and fences, horses, calves and lambs
float helpless by, moaning their last faint cry—
who from despair and loss returned to city's arms
and at the sea gate found a silver ship.

3

Who have loved water, yearned for flood
watched woolly clouds puffed from the piping sky
have held the crumbling firmament in hand
and knew no seeds could breathe, no green life flow;
who on the burnt spring grass cherished a crocus bloom
until we cursed it, for it bore no bread.
Who had no walls, no home
no animals in barn
only the rusted implements
only the thistle, self-sown.
Who trekked bare-footed, underfed
greedy for fruit in Okanagan fields,
thirsty for ocean even if salt it be:
who have paused here, on brink of life again
to build the ships and bless the autumn rain.

4

Who have been reared on rations and soup-kitchens
and sent from school unlearned, clutching at work
riding the rods with hobos, drug fiends, college students
and sleeping, at the country's end, in flophouse—

Who have lain low, known thin girls in alley
kissed under a bridge and pillowed on stone
who raised a fist to window, blind with anger
and demonstrated hate in the streets of the sleek;

Who have been thrown a bone and yapped at thrower
who looked this gift horse sharply in the mouth
who work, watching; who launch ships, wary
waiting the year's turn, living to see. . .
We too are here, bent over bench and caulker
our hearts awake; for now, our voices free.

       He who knew heaven saw the gateway open
       heard the morning singing in the hold.
       He who knew heaven seized a rivet, hammer
       ran to new keel laid on ways, to new life set
       ready for use, ready to break or build.

FINALE

High on our hill we watched, and saw
morning become high noon, and the tide full.
Saw children chequered on the western beach
and ferry boats plough back and forth, knocking the nose
of tugboats, barges, freighters, convoys, cruisers:
the harbour a great world of moving men
geared to their own salvation, taking heart.
We watched gold sun wheel past the sombre park
slip beyond Lion's Gate, illuminate
cool purple skyline of the Island hills.
Then to the hulls and houses silence came
blinds down on tired eyes
dark drew its blanket over trees and streets
grey granaries and harbour lights; muffled the mountain-side.
Yet still, far, far below those lights pierced sky
and water; blue and violet, quick magenta flash
from welder's torch; and still the foreshore roared
strumming the sea, drumming its rhythm hard
beating out strong against the ocean's song:
the graveyard shift still hammering its way
towards an unknown world, straddling new day.

Prophet of the New World
(Begun in 1945; revised since)

Prophet of the New World
A Poem for Voices

CHORUS:

Who is he that comes, treading on hope
Indian footed? Remembering how
when the lean rock pulls winter on its face
natives of the plains know time is near
to hunt the buffalo for hides, for meat
and in thin bush to trap the beaver skin?

Who is he with Ireland in his name
and Scandinavian humour in his veins?
What poet, or what dreamer, caught
in music of his own imagining?
Who is he devout and filial
with the French vowels on his tongue
l'amour de dieu within his heart:

Who is he that comes?

MADAME RIEL:

He is my son. Louis Riel, my son.
His father came from ribboned country, where
the farms run neck and neck to reach the river.
Then he came west, to find the prairie land,
Assiniboia, ruled by Hudson Bay.
He saw good earth and tilled it, built a mill
for Métis and for Indians, hunters of buffalo,
to learn new ways and settle down: *la terre!*
as did those others, white men, a colony
against lean times: the days of drought
the shrill descent of locusts.

Close to the hearth the family warmed our hearts—
Our boy grew strong: a hunter, yet a dreamer.
And bolder grew his questions, till we had
no knowledge left to give him. So we sent him east
to converse with the priests, perhaps to be
a son of theirs, not ours—

Until one day, my good man's life went out.
I was alone with children still to raise. The crops!
The sheep and cattle dying.
A letter sent to Montreal struck the boy's heart.
He would come home, forget about book learning—
What did *that* matter, if his people called?
He would come home.

LOUIS RIEL:

I dreamed two dreams.
Once, as a child, out on my father's riverbank
tending the sheep.
Huddled close, their woolly dumbness sensed
the wind was whistling for October. Beast to beast
they looked towards each other for a place to turn
but all being faint of heart, stayed close.
Then I grew cold, and crouched among them
my head shoved down between their warming fleece;
my heart
seemed to be beating in slow time with theirs
under the wind, in the brittle grass.

And then—
O then I heard my name called out aloud!
I raised my eyes and saw day brighten
like a sword—
till all the air was stinging with white light.

"The sheep are leaderless" my own voice spoke.

"The sheep have chosen you," another cried:
for you are *Exovede—from the flock!*
One of them! Without authority except through them.
From the flock you must go out, there where my children are
as speechmaker and peacemaker; you must be voice
for them, for Me."

I looked, but saw no thing.
Only the first snow, whirling down.
Then darkness came.
I woke, my body stiff
from huddling with the sheep.

First, I was cold; and then,
hearing The Voice, in my mind,
I was become on fire!
Afterwards the farm, its ways, its work
enfolded me. I dropped down into sleep.
I was a child again.

MADAME RIEL:

Then came the years you went away to school
to be a priest, we hoped...
Then, was it not, you dreamed
your second dream, my son?

RIEL:

I dreamed we wrestled in a wood—my Lord
with flaming tomahawk, his mind afire
and I slow animal with limbs of man
battling the light. I, crying to be known
by him, delivering fierce blows for truth
to shake my chains in helplessness—
I, pitted small against his towering
saw his blood spurt and bruises burst like flowers:
downfallen to the earth his armour lay.

Then cried out in my pity: "Lord, forgive."
And as I stooped, he was a-sudden over me
his feathers fire, his body like a blade
and I it was who bruised and streaming lay
and woke up knocking at my breast and bone...
a lonely man, but truth unfettering me!
Here on this earth to fight for freedom's light,
here in this flowered land to end the hate.

MADAME RIEL:

So. So must it be... Tell no one, son.
They 'll call you mad, for sure.
Tell no one of your dream.

CHORUS:

Full of foreboding and dark; from the dark we come
suffer a little; and into the dark go.
A door closes; a sign is up, For Sale;
the hand loved garden is smothered over with weeds
daffodils plunge wilder into the wild wood
earth quickly erases where human footprint trod
and the will of man becomes but the wind's way.

Shall it all go back, return?
Earth to her ancient privilege,
city to ash, the future skyscrapers
choked in a desperate struggle for air?
Shall the plane crash, and the sky fall
and the heart that beat so wildly be muffled
its meaning merged into the massing dark?

RIEL:

Mad, did she say mad? Madness is
the meat of poetry; and every poet's mad
who has a message burning in his bowels.
Say I am mad; say that the slowly turning world
rifled with hate, red skin against white
fathers perverting sons, and all of nature made
into a kitchen midden for man's wasteful heart—
call these things *sane*? and their existence, *bliss*?
Still I am mad, who would destroy and burn
the shame of racial hate; I, the half-caste
neither white nor brown, am therefore mad:
more human, less possessed of bigotry
nearer, I feel, to the great God who came
to be amongst us, flesh, to feel
the animal passions of this creature, man.
Make me more mad, dear Father! that beyond
the barriers of everyday, my Soul
may plunge; and so, forever be on fire
a comet flashing faith upon the world.

MADAME RIEL:

So, he returned to us; to Winnipeg.
Eighteen hundred and sixty-nine
he fought the fight—
gave to the untitled, the squatters
land that the Hudson's Bay
had held for Company spoils—
"a skin for a skin" their motto.
Our Louis ripped off the "HBC"
from the Company's flag
and let the good nuns of St. Boniface
sew, in its place, the one word, "Nation."
Together we created
the Provisional Government
of Assiniboia
and in eighteen hundred and seventy-three
elected Louis Riel as our representative
to Parliament at Ottawa!
But instead of being allowed to take his seat
he, my son
was charged with the killing of Thomas Scott
by a firing squad, at Fort Garry.
The rights and wrongs of *that*
will be argued for many a year. . .
But Louis Riel escaped by boat down the river
and fled across the border—
officially at Ottawa they said
"banished from his own country."

RIEL:

Even an exile must keep busy, work,
forget to dream. I swept aside
all purpose other than to follow on
the turn of seasons; and to shield with love
my little ones— my wife and little ones.

MADAME RIEL:

Then, the eighteen eighties; news abroad
talk coming from the north, of hunger
and starvation in Saskatchewan;
infringement of the rights
of Métis and of Frenchmen; the native-born
and newcome pioneer both restless grown
at the indifference of the Government.

RIEL:

It came by word of mouth, an endless chain
of words, from farm to farm—
until one day dust clogged our narrow road
and clopping horses drowned the sparrow's chirp.
Two horsemen galloped up, alighted at my door—
men of brownish skin and straight brown hair
their faces known to me in dreams—
two messengers from Métis friends
calling me home across the line, to give
my wit and wisdom to their cause;
asking for aid as leader of their flock:
I, Exovede—*from their flock!* Because I knew
with my experience, how to speak well
the tongue of governments; how to set forth our rights
yet offer, still in peace, the other cheek.

I listened. Then I prayed.
And then I came.
Back to the heartland that had nourished me.

CHORUS:

What particular dream, what sad report
from the country across the chasm
does he bring, the stranger—
he whom we had almost forgotten?

Has he a name still, has he dyed his hair
or is he still exuberant and bold
and what is his news, what manner of wonders
will he propound? Will he confound us?

Look, he has changed his clothes
altered his manner of speaking:
in his gait he limps, he walks with an arm uplifted.
Is he therefore still one of us? Can he be called ours?
And do we want him?

O there is the nub of the question!
Will he hold us, spurning, until he has told all
until silence spreads like early sunlight
over and into the grass, through the wood's crannies
under the leaves, under the tight skin?

Hush. He is mounting the rostrum:
be silent, stop questioning, hold yourselves ready.
Hush, for his lips are open. His words hurl truth.

RIEL:

Le Canada pour les Canadiens!
And who are we, Canadians?
This land is mother to me,
Blood and bone.
Yet like a mother, she has room
for more. Her arms, Red River and Assiniboine,
her arms are empty. The knotty land upthrust,
charred trunk, naked torso of rock
no eyes for sight, no face
shining out of the night—
day, a deep yawn where voice should be—
pure physical, girded with rivers,
boundaried by birds,
mapped by the grooves of buffalo and wolf.
Behold my land! a stride of seven leagues,
a giant pulse! And yet no head,
no tower for the mind.

Therefore she must be peopled.
With French blood, and with the Irish
Scandinavian, Scotch.
Some German stock I'd have—Bavarians, Russians, Poles
and the lone Jew whose face is veiled
with all the mourning of these
eighteen hundred years. Perhaps for him
the waves of the Pacific will chant a sweet
slow music to console his heart.

And what of us? We Métis rooted here
The firstfruits of the country?
Must we go backward, yield, be dispossessed?
Ah no! Not if our temper's yet
what in the past it's been. Remember 1869!
To us who share all willingly with all who come,
to us must come fair share.
I see myself The Prophet of the New World!
The land *was* ours; it shall be
ours and yours.

CHORUS:

Now all is past. The trial
the final passionate
self-defence. The hanging
at Regina.
November 1885 is history.

MADAME RIEL:

We brought his body back to Winnipeg
in a plain wooden box—
then gave him a new coffin
decent burial
in his own earth, at St. Vital.

CHORUS:

Now the dark plunge of the year is done:
we make new prophecies
and stand, unhelmeted
facing remote certainties.
In the mind's eye bare branch
leaps with encircling green—
the pushing, probing blades.
These will be here, come bomb
or barbs of love lost, lost; come fire
to hospital, museum, home.
Over a burnt black sod the grasses grow,
the vine creeps back over the shattered porch:
the ships we built, the mills, the sprawling towns
these our own hands destroy. But not
O never will the grasping claw
reach down, break earth, tear seed from seed!
and never will the child in war, the womb in woman be
made devastate. For green returns
tenacious signal, friend to ambushed eyes.

From Poems for People
(1945-1947)

Page One

Reared on snow she was
Manacled in ice
Ten frostbound winters of her life
In bondage to this Lear
This blue lipped, fondling father
Whose hard chains
Clanked on her feet
Pinched the poor fingers stiff with pain.
Play, an ordeal to be endured
As feathery snow
Festooned the faces
Ridiculed the shapes
A rigid fence
Lay bundled on the hill
And snow made ladies out of trees
Those bare and gangling boys.

Feasted on snow
And cold's glass palaces she knew
The ice yard where huge blocks were river flung
To fortress out a field
And in the corridors of crisp
And rainbow shafted crystal
She traced the pattern of a princess' day
And was her godmother
And listened to her pray.

O might there always be
Those wishes three

That dazzling evanescent dress
Those pearls, those tears
That slipper made of glass—

But not for me.

But not for me
Whistled the winter wisdom of the wind:
The ice that bound her could not be her home
Native this land, but not
The boundary of her home.

2

When spring sneaked sucking at the snow
Its tongue devouring humps and hills
Sipping at icicles until they dripped
In ignominious patter on
The rude brown water barrel's yawn—
Then rivulets began to run
The sound of shovels rasped the air
Grinding on chunks embedded firm
Demanding still a further term;
And in the slush, all sparkle gone
Water began to make its home
To sigh and sing, to crack and swing
Its column in the underground.

At such a moment, such a day
Her head was lifted suddenly
Her ears believed, her heart heard
The sky's hallooing honking word.
Here, in this wasting winter, geese
Briefly for feeding came to rest
Here they were transients, who knew
Some other home lay farther on
Some grass upshaken
A forest to be taken;
And following their arrowed alphabet
Straining to see their jet-
Propulsion through the unstained sky
She felt her feet untried
Her winter thongs unpried.
She was a moving miracle of wing and sound
No one home hers, but all homes to be found.

Inheritance

In the rooms of my mind you pace
Sad parent, your own head thorned—
Not in my power to bestow or bless
No gesture for surcease.

Some silence there was: sun's fierce
Assertion on a windy height,
Some daylight peace. But none to pierce
Shouting abyss, and raving night.

They called you shy; a blusterer—
Two poles, stretched agony between
And some might wonder why the grass grew green
Where acid words had lately been.

In the rooms of my heart you race
Fiery father of us, your kind,
Your burdened brood; who yet will face
The day, the dark; housed in a quiet mind.

Preludium

The infant, like an invalid,
Is slow aware of worlds to win.
At first the lifting of a hand
Is gasping effort; and the clutch at cloth
Releases rhythm and delight
Till day blows when the body prone
Is propped, by inner urge is prodded vertical
And balanced on firm flesh. To sit alone
Is an essential bliss we know again
After long illness, close to death. . . .

Until, O upright man, to cast off animal
To stand on tingling toes and balance there one's loved
One's certain self—supreme self-consciousness!

And if the tower builded then
Be bold and venturesome
Not all negations, whippings, snares
Not all the frantic obstacles to face
Can down the darer, hold the hurler here
From swaddling clothes or shroud—
O listen loud
Hear Hercules ascending to his height:
Behold the towering portent, Man alone!

The Mother

She cannot walk alone. Must set her pace
To the slow count of grasses, butterflies,
To puppy's leap, the new bulldozer's wheeze
To Chinese fishman, balancing his pole.

She cannot think alone. Words must be
Poised to the smaller scope, immediates
Of wagon's broken wheel, a battered knee,
The sun's high promise for a day of play.

And when the active hours are gone, it's still
Her lot to busily bestir herself
With knots and nooses, all the slough and slips
Of day. When evening's seal is set she must

Have chosen here to stay. To sit, to hear
The day's confessions eased from tired tongue,
To soothe the small lids down to drowsiness
Till childhood sleep perfumes the darkened room.

Small Fry

Their cries
Rise and recede
As hills by train
Heave huge and blot the sky
Shrill with demand
Then fall and fan
Into the muted ripples of a plain.

Their talk
Is bird brief, irresponsible
The answer asked
Not waited for
And the word punched
Back like a volley ball.

Their song is man's
Own early voice
Heart free and eased
Throat seized
With tremors of light
Sun's scale from branch to branch
Storming delight.

Abracadabra
for Peter at Halloween

In the wicked afternoon
When the witch is there
When night's downsnare
Swoops like a loon
Strafing the air
In the wicked afternoon

In the witty time of day
When the mind's at play
The cat's at call
The guitar off the wall
Wind holds sway
In the witty time of day

Then the witch will walk
Full of witty talk
And the cat will stalk
Tail high as a cock

The guitar in the room
Will fuss and fume
Strumming at the tune
For a wicked afternoon
And out in the park
Wind will unfrock
The autumn trees
And falling leaves
Shiver with shock.

And time with his
Weaving, wailing horn
Shivers my timbers
Shatters my corn:
Little boy blue
Blows a blue tune
On a wicked afternoon.

Carnival

1

The winged wheels whirr
A hemisphere
Of gaudy speed
Onlookers jeer
At safety's door
While the perilous
Pilot's tale
Is lost in his
Soul saving wail.

The wheels of time
Whirl and climb
Leap the loop
Swoop at the sun
Then slacken, droop:
Till web is spun
And travel's done.

2

Here cornucopia
Calls the tune
To rhythm of
A clowning croon

Cacophony of can
Tin pan,
The yodel and
The ragtime man.

And for your thirst
The usual punches
Synthetic syrup
Hotdog lunches

Ambrosial foam
Is offered—pink
Enough to make
The palate shrink

Along with kewpies,
Guns and cushions
Enough to
Educate the Russians.

Above the din
The showman's heckle
Offers you heaven
For a nickel.

3

Save me a little
Silver wheel
A chariot swung
On the world's reel

Save me a time
No hour counts
No clock warns
No minute mounts

Hammock me high
In breathless bliss
To swaying mountains
Speed's kiss

And drop me lifeless
To the ground
The song forever
Lost in sound.

4

*So said the little boy
Alone
To the keeper with
The toy throne:*

Please mount me on
That glittering river
Where the lights leap gold
At the sky's quiver

And set my boat
A-whirling in
That tortuous tunnel
Dark within

And save me when
Inside that cave
The engines stop
And no one's brave

But swallowed up
The heart and soul
A thousand turnings
From the goal—

When power's off
And lights are blown
And all the easy
Laughing's gone

Save me from
That tinsel start
The phony thunder
Of my heart!

Guide me towards
An open door
Where daylight dazzles
Every pore

And where the breath
At first uneven
Wings the body
Down from heaven.

So said the little boy
Alone
To the keeper of
The toy throne.

Of Mourners

Mourn not for man, speeding to lay waste
The essence of a countryside's most chaste
And ageless contour; her cool-breasted hills,
Purled streams, bare choirs in wood, fair daffodils—

Mourn not, as maudlin singers did, the scars
Left by the slag, industrial wars,
Men tearing fields apart for railway towns
Wresting the silly sheep from sleepy downs:

And sing no more the sentimental song
Of spinning jenny holding lads too long,
Of children toiling underground, or laws
For hanging witches, burning corn for cause.

Sing only with the gibing Chaucer's tongue
Of foible and grave fault; of words unsung,
More pungent victory than battles won:
Sing deeds neglected, desecrations done

Not on the lovely body of the world
But on man's building heart, his shaping soul.
Mourn, with me, the intolerant, hater of sun:
Child's mind maimed before he learns to run.

In Time of War

You went, wordless; but I had not the will
Nor courage to find fanciful or plumaged phrase
To camouflage my solitude. So saying bald
Good-bye, word bouncing down each waiting step
Till out of sight and sound, I saw you turn
Walk firm toward the iron gate. Its clang
Shattered a world. For should we greet again
This hushed horizon will have widened so
You'll not find solace walking in the Park
Or watching storm snarl over English Bay.
That night of fog, bleaching the bones of trees
Will not shroud you and me again; too wide apart
We will have grown; our thoughts too proud
Too tall for sheltering beneath these boughs.

You knew the secret wood. Absorbed
Its effortless surrender into spring:
Pink cameo pinned on a furred stem,
Hepatica; then bloodroot's waxen wing.

You knew green shadow, sunburnt shade
Heat's parasol impersonal
The dried stream and the bare brown stone
Thrush's reiterated call.

Maple you saw, bursting in tongues of flame—
The yellowed birch leaves' flashing fan,
Wind resilient; and oaks' rust brown
Hugging the bough since summer ran.

O what a winter is there now
For us who, separate, have known
Blood on the snow this year! Disaster's news
Ripping the sky where geese had flown.

3

Confused, embedded, over-turbulent world
Whirling and swarming on outboard passage—
In space churning; in ether resounding
Never ceaseless; never without sound.

They say there is centre, cavern of calm
For no hearing; no sounding jeer
They say in a muffled underworld
Quiet is born for the inner ear.

Not knowing is not finding. But some—
That soldier newly come
Wears such silence on his face:
He has been to that place.

Not death, though he know its beak
Not sleep, that cup for thirst.
Agony swept him, flak burst
The punctured sky made shriek:

And eyes failing, ears dim
Voluptuous the quiet came.
Tensed on the nerves of silence, he:
That soldier standing quietly.

4

It seemed a poor thing to do, to wed, when the Japanese
Had begun to gnaw their way through the Manchu
      plains,
When Spain cast a ballot, and was outraged, raped
In an olive grove, by a monastery wall.
It seemed no time for love, when the hands
Idled in empty pockets and coffee was five cents a cup.
It seemed no time to lie down in a clearing
At sundown, with the woodcutters gone, and the thrush's
Voice fluting the firs. But you said: "Have faith."
You said, "Only Hitler was in a hurry and his haste
Would one day be spent." So you said. And we wed.

Now it is eight years after, to the day, to the hour:
The wrath has devoured itself and the fire eaten the fire.
And again at sundown over the bird's voice, low
Over the firs fluted with evening I hear the Yangtse flow
And the rubble of Barcelona is this moss under my hand.

London Revisited: 1946

I

In the cavern of cold
Chill of the world
Turn of the old
Year's leaf to the soil
September to sere
In the cave of the year

The long fingered wall
Of the house disembowelled
Stares in a prayer
Voiceless, unvowelled:
Inerasably stained
The stone is unveiled.

(But down in the pit
Where the cellar was hit
It is green, it is gold:
From the grass and leaf mould
Willow herb's knit
With goldenrod's hold.)

In the cave of the year
The underground ride
Heart knocks in fear
Map is no guide—
Whose is this hand
Chained to your side?

Once it was death's. We saw
The bone of the beast
Stretcher bearer's torch
Flashed on his dark feast

Once in the tense sky
Riveted with blood
We visioned blank defeat
The iron flood

Had not our prophets cried
Ruin! No release!
And politicians lied
Predicting peace?

Now in the surging street
Sway and sweep of song
It is not death whose arm
Hurries us along

It is not death, for that
We met with a proud smile
Tossing a hand grenade
At the rocket's snarl

It is not death, but he
We feared, we fled:
Our brother, searching us—
Love's lightning tread.

Coming upon this face as to a map
Learning the contours not from street to street
But from the coloured ink, the gay red arteries
The yellow wrinkles and the shaded brow:
Coming to London with an eager now
The printed Golders dancing on the Green
The happy Shepherds hunting in the Bush
Coming to Chelsea and the brush
Of autumn tarnishing a square
(Whether a sheltered court, demure, austere
Or narrow alley where the children flare
Their whittled voices on the nipping air)—

Coming with guide and gift, I fell
Blundering through dark, around
No builded wall
I fell and heard my fall
Echoing through the tall
Rubble of rift and wreck
Down to the low unreaching wretched wall
Through the last door hung
On naked nail
And the stairs flung
Up to the gap of hell:
And above, no ceiling
And below, no wall.

4

O feet that found the way to bed,
The narrow place where prayers were said;
That danced a circle on the floor
And kicked a hollow on the door

O feet that morning noon and night
Suffered the hour to be delight
Or stood upon the edge of mist
And felt the earth, and met, and kissed—

Into the parapet of time
Memorial tower of the mind
You have ascended in a climb
Sudden as a flying bomb

You have left the city's face
Scarred and grimed by human hand
And all the magic of her map
Crumbling in brick and sand.

And though the Michaelmas is here
A mauve repose on mildewed stain
And children swing on girders grown
Rusty with the wrack of rain

And though the mushroom houses grow
In prim, prefabricated row;
Where debris was, a park will be
And here a chaste community—

Still lies the skeleton behind,
The bony manufactured grin
The voice we heard time out of mind
That rustles when the leaves are thin;

And still the footprints trace the map
Scuttle across the veins and flaws
Reverberating on the heart
To warn the way that winter was.

Improvisation on an Old Theme

If I must go, let it be easy, slow
The curve complete, and a sure swerve
To the goal. Let it be slow and sweet
To know how leaf consumes its time,
How petal sucks to the sun's heat
Or as old bones, settling into soil,
Eyes too remote for earth's light
Set on a solar circle whose bright
Business brims the universe.

Let me know well how the winds blow
Smoky in autumn with leaf reek;
And summer's sleek surrender,
Torching the maple; let my branches sigh
For snow, and in a muffled mantle, let me go.

Keep me for quiet. Save me ever from
Disastrous ending sounding without drum,
No decent exhalation of the breath—
The dazzling violence of atomic death.

Lullaby

Till the end of our time
Let the forests and fronds
Of my dream
Be background for
Words from the heart outsprung
A fountain song:

Let the quick of your hands
Be arteries that lead
Through valleyed hills
Staying in love
At stations of unrest—
The quick of your hands
To the quick of me.

Let me be patient earth
To your leaning sky
Whether the sun fills
Or you are emptied cool
With only an austere moon
To lighten me,

Let me be hushed at last
As the world sleeps, turning
From its own nightmare; the begging child
Ruined in fear
Turning forever away
From the jocular grin of the side-stepping wall
The woman's arm
In the rubble fall.

Let me sleep at last
Who groan as the earth creaks over
Its own disasters
Let me close my eyes forever against
The map on my wall
Let me be silent and still
Stop up my ears to blur
The child's cruel cry at my sill.
Drug and dope me, dress me with love's fine hand
Till the end of our time.

Autumn in Wales

In the museum
Our day stood still
With the cool
Statues, the folded word
Butterfly wing and tongue of bird
All in the glass case held and heard.

We saw ourselves
Together in time:
The corridors
Were mirrors of
Our own revolving
Echoing selves. Hearing our hearts
Eyes swept
Beyond each other
To the far halls
The stately stairs
And the ornaments.

(Familiar as
A falling word
This unspoken
Intimate
Appraisal of
The other there:
We could not look
Nor even care
To touch:
This was the plunge
We took.)

For behind the cool
Immaculate wall
Your valleys lay:
The brown laced bracken
Of the common
Sheep rust red, and the hill
Helmeted with tawny elm.

Behind the solemn
Waterfall,
A tall column,
Lay valleys dark
And walled with home
A cottage tiled
And roofed with fire
And hill's high arm.

And past the archways
And relics still
Arrayed in stone
There the gateways
Built of the cliff's bone
Secretly guarding
The sea's ascent
And lash of its foaming
Firmament.

Gnarled and irregular
The Welsh cliff's fold
Wild the indentation of the wind
And your voice whispering the wind's
Insistent word—
Loud in my heart
And yet unheard.

O valley of autumn
Museum of one day
White cliff and column
Shattering in spray

Hold here familiar
Or strange meeting-place:
Green hills be walls
Forever shaping us.

From Call My People Home
(1948-1950)

Call My People Home
(A Documentary Poem for Radio)

ANNOUNCER:

Now after thirty years come from a far island
Of snow and cherry blossoms, holy mountains,
To make a home near water, near
The blue Pacific; newcomers and strangers
Circled again and shaped by snow-white mountains,
These put down their roots, the Isseis: *
The older generation. This is their story.

CHORUS OF ISSEIS:

Home, they say, is where the heart is:
Transplanted walls, and copper-coloured gardens
Or where the cherry bough can blow
Against your pain, and blow it cool again—
This they call home.

But for ourselves we learned
How home was not
Even the small plot, raspberry laden
Nor shack on stilts, stooping over the water,
Nor the brown Fraser's whirl,
Sucking the salmon upward.

Home was the uprooting:
The shiver of separation,
Despair for our children
Fear for our future.

Home was the finding of a dry land
Bereft of water or rainfall
Where water is cherished
Where our tears made channels
And became irrigation.

*Isseis—generation born in Japan.

Home was in watching:
The fruit growing and pushing
So painfully watered;
The timber hewn down
The mill run completed.

Home was in waiting:
For new roots holding
For young ones branching
For our yearning fading. . .

ANNOUNCER:

His ancestors had lived near water
Been fishermen under Fujiyama's shadow.
Each season in the new land found him struggling
Against the uncertain harvest of the sea,
The uncertain temper of white fishermen
Who hungered also, who had mouths to feed.
So these men cut his share
From half to one-eighth of the fishing fleet:
But still he fished, finding the sea his friend.

THE FISHERMAN:

Home was my boat: T.K. 2930—
Wintering on the Skeena with my nets
Cast up and down the river, to lure and haul
The dogfish. (His oil, they said, was needed overseas
For children torn from home, from a blitzed town.)
We made good money, and the sockeye run
That summer had outdone all the remembered seasons.
Now I could own my boat, *Tee Kay,* the Gillnetter
The snug and round one, warm as a woman
With her stove stoked at night and her lanterns lit
And anchor cast, brooding upon the water
Settled to sleep in the lap of the Skeena.

Now after thirty years, come from an island
To make a home near water: first on a sailing vessel
Towed, each season, to the fishing grounds:
Then the small gasboat, the gillnetter, that belonged
Not to the man who fished, but to the cannery.
Now after thirty years a free man, naturalized,
A man who owned his boat! I smelt the wind
Wetting my face, waves dashing against the *Tee Kay*'s
    sides
The grey dawn opening like a book
At the horizon's rim. I was my own master—
Must prove it now, today! Stooping over the engine
Priming the starter, opening the gas valve,
I felt her throbbing in answer; I laughed
And grasped the fly wheel, swung her over.
She churned off up the river—my own boat, my home.

That was before Pearl Harbor: before a December day
Spent on a restless sea; then anchor in the dusk
And down to bunk to have a bowl of rice.
By lantern light I turned the battery set
To hear brief messages from fishermen
From boat to shore, to learn the weather forecast.
Must have been dozing when I woke up sharp—
What was he saying? Some kind of government order?
"All fishing craft on the high seas must head at once
To the nearest port, report to authorities."
Did they not want our fish, the precious oil?
"No," said the voice, "Our boats were to be examined, searched
For hidden guns, for maps, for treachery. . . ."
I heard, but could not understand. Obeyed,
But as a blind man. The numb fear about my boat,
Tee Kay, found no release in port, off shore,
Rubbing against a fleet of trollers, frail gillnetters
All heading down for Inverness and Tusk
All in the dark, with rumour flying fast.
No one knew more than his fear whispered,
No one explained.
We thought: perhaps it's all a mistake
Perhaps they'll line us up and do a search
Then leave us free for Skeena, Ucluelet—
The time is ripe, the season's fish are running.

There was no mistake. It wasn't a joke:
At every fishing port more boats fell in.
Some had no wood, no gasoline; and some
Barely a day's store of food aboard.
So we waited at the Inlet's mouth, till the 16th.

How speak about the long trip south, the last
We ever made, in the last of our boats?
The time my life turned over, love went under
Into the cold unruly sea. Those waves
Washing the cabin's walls
Lashed hate in me.

We left Rupert in two long lines of sixty boats
Strung to the seiners, met and tugged
By *Starpoint* and the naval escort, the corvette.
All day we watched the gloomy sea roughed up
By westerlies, but had to tough it out
Glued to the wheel, weary for sleep, till 2 a.m.

Then, at Lowe Inlet, had brief anchorage.
At Milbanke Sound we ran into heavier seas
The buffeted boats like so many bobbing corks
Strung on a thin rope line that over and over
Would break, be mended by the corvette's men
And then again be snapped by snarling sea.

Day merged into night and day again
Found us with six boats broken loose; some torn
And others gashed with bumping in the dark—
If some drugged fisherman fell off to sleep
And left craft pilotless,
Smashing like blind birds through a log-strewn sea.
Some boats that had no gasoline to keep
Heart thumping in their engines, these
Were plucked aloft in fistfuls by the waves
Then brought down with a thud—
Propellers spinning helpless in mid-air.
So we proceeded into colder, rougher seas,
Seasick and sore, nodding at the wheel,
Then stamping up and down to keep the winter out.

Christmas at sea. The bitterest for me
That any year had given. Even so
Some had a celebration, pooled their funds
And bought the only chicken left in Alert Bay.
Others boiled cabbages in salt sea water,
Pulled out the playing cards and shrugged, and laughed.
As we set sail at midnight, now a thousand boats
Chained to the naval escort, steadily south
Into familiar waters where the forests cooled their feet
At rocks'-end, mountains swam in mist—
As we set sail for home, the young ones, born here, swore
Not softly, into the hissing night. The old men wept.

The rest takes little telling. On the fifteenth night
We passed Point Grey's low hulk, our long line wavered
    shoreward.
Dirty and hungry, sleep lying like a stone
Stuck in our heads, we nosed our broken craft
Into the wharf at Steveston, "Little Tokyo."
The crowd on the dock was silent. Women finding their men
Clung to them searchingly, saying never a word,
Leading them home to the *ofuro** and supper.
Others of us, like me, who knew no one,
Who had no place near the city's centre
Stood lonely on the wharf, holding the *Tee Kay*'s line
For the last time, watching the naval men
Make a note of her number, take my name.
That was the end of my thirty years at the fishing
And the end of my boat, my home.

ANNOUNCER:

These their children, the Niseis,† were born
Into the new world, called British Columbia home,
Spoke of her as mother, and beheld
Their future in her pungent evergreen.

---

*Ofuro—the bath.
†Niseis—generation born in Canada.

A YOUNG NISEI:

We lived unto ourselves
Thinking so to be free
Locked in the harbour
Of father and mother
The children incoming
The tide inflowing.

Sometimes at remote midnight
With a burnt-out moon
An orange eye on the river
Or rising before dawn
From a house heavy with sleepers
The man touching my arm
Guiding my hand through the dark
To the boat softly bumping and sucking
Against the wharf;
We go out toward misty islands
Of fog over the river
Jockeying for position;
Till morning steals over, sleepy,
And over our boat's side, leaning
The word comes, Set the nets!
Hiding the unannounced prayer
Resounding in the heart's corners:
May we have a high boat
And the silver salmon leaping!

We lived unto ourselves
Locked in the harbour

I remember the schoolhouse, its battered doorway
The helter-skelter of screaming children
Where the old ones went, my sisters
Soberly with books strapped over their shoulders:
Deliberately bent on learning—

(And learned, soon enough, of
The colour of their skin, and why
Their hair would never turn golden.)

But before the bell rang
For me
My turn at becoming
Before the bell rang
I was out on the hillside
Reaching high over my head for the black ones
The first plump berries of summer;
A scratch on the arm, maybe, a tumble
But filling my pail and singing my song
With the bees humming
And the sun burning.

Then no bell rang for me;
Only the siren.
Only the women crying and the men running.
Only the Mounties writing our names
In the big book; the stifled feeling
Of being caught, corralled.
Only the trucks and a scramble to find
A jacket, a ball, for the bundle.

My blackberries spilled
Smeared purple
Over the doorway.
Never again did I go
Blackberry picking on the hillside.
Never again did I know
That iron schoolbell ringing.

The children incoming
The tide inflowing.

ANNOUNCER:

From the upper islands of the coast
With only one day's notice to depart
Came these, and hundreds like them: Mariko and her
        mother.
In the re-allocation centre, Hastings Park
Mariko writes a letter.

I wonder where in the inner country
On what train shooting between two mountains
You fly tonight, Susumu?
When I explain to you how it is here
You will understand, perhaps,
Why I have not been able to tell my mother
About you and me.

It is this: she is continually frightened—
Never having lived so, in a horse stall before.
My bunk is above hers, and all night I lie rigid
For fear to disturb her; but she is disturbed.
She has hung her pink petticoat from my bunk rail
Down over her head, to be private; but nothing is private.
Hundreds of strangers lie breathing around us
Wakeful, or coughing; or in sleep tossing;
Hundreds of strangers pressing upon us
Like horses tethered, tied to a manger.

My mother lies wakeful with her eyes staring.
I cannot see her, but I know. She is thinking:
This is a nightmare. She is back in her home
Embroidering blossoms on a silk kimono
Talking to me of Yosh (the boy I mentioned,
The one I grew up with). She is making plans
To visit the go-between; to bake for a wedding.

My mother cannot believe her dream is over,
That she lies in a manger with her hands tethered.
So you will understand now, Susumu:
I have not been able to tell my mother.
It is hard for me to believe, myself,
How you said the words, how you spoke of a garden
Where my name, MARIKO, would be written in
    flowers. . . .
I wonder where in the inner country
On what train far from this animal silence
This thick night stifling my heart, my nostrils—
Where like a rocket shooting between two planets
Have you flown, Susumu? Have you gone?

ANNOUNCER:

Between the fury and the fear
The window-breaking rabble and the politician's
    blackout,
(Wartime panic fed
On peacetime provocations)
Between the curfew rung
On Powell Street
And the rows of bunks in a public stable
Between the line-ups and the labels and the presentation
    of a one-way ticket
Between these, and the human heart—
There was in every centre one man, a white man—
A minister, a layman—a mayor.

THE MAYOR:

That year the snow came early, lay lightly on our hills
Cooling their colours, pointing up the evergreen
Scribbled over the ledges; at valley's end
Snow muffled with its mantle the gaunt shape,
The smokeless chimney of the copper smelter.

I stood on the station platform reading the message
Telegraphed from Vancouver: "The first contingent,
Sixty-eight persons, arriving on the night train."
Then I looked down our narrow, funnelled valley
My ghost-town village, with hotels closed up
Since gold-rush days; post office perched
Upon a down-hill lurch, leaning towards empty stores.

Sixty-eight persons, and where could they find a pillow?
The government shacks were only half completed,
Without heat or water; there remained a hotel
Half boarded up; a church; some vacant houses
Left tenantless, standing on back streets.
These I tried first; but the neighbours protested:
They had read the newspapers, they did not want
Criminals and spies settling upon their doorsteps.
There was nothing for it but to open the creaking door,
Put stoves and straw in the Golden Gate Hotel.

At seven-fifteen the evening train pulled in.
I stood alone on the platform, waiting.
Slowly the aliens descended, in huddled groups,
Mothers and crying children; boys and girls
Holding a bundle of blankets, cardboard boxes,
A basket of pots and pans, a child's go-cart—
Looking bewildered up and down the platform,
The valley closing in, the hostile village. . . .

I stepped forward, urged into sudden action.
The women cowered, fell back, cried words
In panic to the old men standing surly, helpless.
I collared a young kid, bright, with his eyes snapping:
"You there, you speak English?" "Why, yah! You bet."
We eyed each other, and I smiled. "You see,"
I said, "I'm mayor here . . . your mayor.
This is your home. Can you tell the people that?
Tell them I'm here to meet them, get acquainted,
Find a place for them to sleep." The boy
Nodded. "Okay, I'll tell my mother, sure.
The rest will believe whatever she says to do."

Their conference began. I waited, tense;
Then plunged into the job of lifting crates
And scanty furnishings, getting local lads
To pile it up on trucks; until I felt
A timid touch upon my arm; I turned
And saw the Issei mother.
                              Putting out my hand
I felt hers move, rest for a moment in mine—
Then we were free. We began to work together.

I remember the long looks of my neighbours
As I strode down the street the next morning
Arm in arm with a flock of Japanese kids.
I took them into the store, the post-office,
Showed them the ropes, then headed for the school,
If no one else in the town would say "hello"
There was one who would!   I knew her
Inside out, like a book—the Principal.

In an hour's time she had them behind desks
Those six, of high school age, those slant-eyed
Black-haired, half-terrified children.
Then I went out to find some carpenters
To build a village in a single day. . . .
It was cold. Light snow covered the hills.
By spring, I vowed, those people would be mine!
This village would be home.

ANNOUNCER:

These were the fathers, mothers, those
Who had to choose another home, another way.
What would they choose? The questioner
Paused with his pencil lifted; gave them a day
To talk together, choose.

THE WIFE:

Either to be a ghost in mountain towns
Abandoned by the fabulous, the seekers
After gold, upon whose bones the forest and the rock
Had feasted; there to sit
With idle hands embroidering the past
Upon a window pane, fed on foreign food
And crowded together in government huts
The men torn from our arms, the family parted,
Or to face the longer, stranger journey
Over the mountain ranges, barred from the sea—
To labour in uncertain soil, inclement weather
Yet labour as one—all the family together?

We looked at each other, you and I, after
So many doubtful years binding our struggles:
Our small plot grown to wider green
Pastured within the Fraser's folds, the shack
Upbuilded to a cottage, now a house—
The cherry trees abloom and strawberry fields
White with the snow of blossom, of promise.

Had it all to be done again, worked at again
By our gnarled hands, in a harsh new land
Where summer passes like a quick hot breath
And winter holds you chained for half the year?
You took my hands, and said: "It's the children's country.
Let them choose." They chafed for independence
Scenting the air of freedom in far fields.
Therefore we had no choice, but one straight way:
The eastward journey into emptiness,
A prairie place called home.

It was harder than hate. Home was a blueprint only.
We lived in a hen coop perched on a farmer's field
Soaked by the sudden storms, the early rains of April.
Yet there was time for ploughing, time to sow
Beet seed upon the strange black soil in rows
Of half an acre; we saw in neighbouring fields'
Bleak tableland, the stabbing green
Of the young wheat; and heard the sweet
Heart-snaring song of meadow-larks; in grass
Withered and brown saw maps move, empty patches
Purple with crocus underneath our feet.

In summer the sun's beak
Tore at our backs bending over the rows
Endless for thinning; the lumpy soil left callouses
Upon our naked knees; mosquitoes swarmed
In frenzied choruses above our heads
Sapping the neck; until a hot wind seared
The field, drove them away in clouds.

I think we had nearly given up, and wept
And gone for government help, another home—
Until, one evening lull, work done
You leaned upon the poplar gate to watch
A lime green sky rim the mauve twilight
While in the pasture fireflies danced
Like lanterns of Japan on prairie air.

Leaning the other way spoke our new friend
The neighbour from the Ukraine;
Touching your arm, using words more broken
Than yours, like scraps of bread left over.

"See how tomorrow is fine. You work
Hard, same as me. We make good harvest time."
He came from a loved land, too, the mild
Plains of the Dneiper where, in early spring
(He said) the violets hid their sweetness. "This land
Is strange and new. But clean and big
And gentle with the wheat. For children too,
Good growing."
He lifted up his hands, his praise; we heard
Over the quickening fields a fresh wind blowing.

ANNOUNCER:

This one was young, a renegade. He wanted the world
In his two hands. He would not make the choice,
But cast it back in their teeth.

NISEI VOICE:

They can't do this to me, Shig said
(Once a Jap, always a Jap)
Why, I went to school with those kids
Vancouver's my home town.

They can't do this to me, Shig said
(Once a Jap, always a Jap)
I'll spend my life in a road camp
In a freight car bunk in the bush.

They'll get tired of me, Shig said
(Once a Jap, always a Jap)
And some dark night I'll buckle my belt
And hitch-hike to the sea.

The Mounties won't get me, Shig said
(Once a Jap, always a Jap)
I'll say I'm a Chinese, see?
It's the underworld for me.

They picked Shig up on a robbery charge
(Once in jail, always in jail)
There were only a few of us such as he
But he blackened our name
Shut the gates to the sea.

ANNOUNCER:

This one was young; but he wanted the world
For others. A philosopher,
He accepted the blow, Pearl Harbor.
He learned the way of waiting.

THE PHILOSOPHER:

To be alone is grace; to see it clear
Without rancour; to let the past be
And the future become. Rarely to remember
The painful needles turning in the flesh.

(I had looked out of the schoolroom window
And could not see the design, held dear
Of the shaken maples; nor the rain, searing and stinging
The burning rain in the eye.

I could not see, nor hear my name called:
Tatsuo, the Pythagoras theorem!
I could not think till the ruler rapped
On the desk, and my mind snapped.

The schoolroom faded, I could not hold
A book again in my hand.
It was the not knowing; the must be gone
Yet the continual fear of going.

Yes, to remember is to go back; to take
The path along the dyke, the lands of my uncle
Stretching away from the river—
The dykeside where we played

Under his fruit trees, canopied with apples,
Falling asleep under a hedgerow of roses
To the gull's shrill chatter and the tide's recurrent
Whisper in the marshland that was home. . . .)

So must I remember. It cannot be hid
Nor hurried from. As long as there abides
No bitterness; only the lesson learned
And the habit of grace chosen, accepted.

CHORUS OF NISEIS:

Home, we discover, is where life is:
Not Manitoba's wheat
Ontario's walled cities
Nor a B. C. fishing fleet.

Home is something more than harbour—
Than father, mother, sons;
Home is the white face leaning over your shoulder
As well as the darker ones.

Home is labour, with the hand and heart,
The hard doing, and the rest when done;
A wider sea than we knew, a deeper earth,
A more enduring sun.

Variations on a Tree

I

Confined to a narrow place
This consciousness, the Word
Is my predicament to be
Separate, yet joined,
Single, yet twain,
Twined in the ancestry of roots
Yet roving in the upper space.

Or are there roots
Seeking to soak themselves in cloud
Crying to the Lord aloud
Stretching out for sustenance
Towards the sun's own countenance?
Invert the world: Now see it roll
Lightly on my palms,
And I immeasurably deep
Wading in pools of blue
Dance branches in eternity
Play football with the moon.

2

Tree falls in foam
On a far shore
Spilling its coins
On the green floor

An aspen bridge
The tightrope where
My childhood walks—
No room to spare.

But Island gained
Was world well lost,
No seething heat,
No stiffening frost,

Into your arms
Tossed at last;
Branches of silence
Consign the past.

3

The tree is Ego, yet
Leaning towards another
With mystery the same;
These twain are brother.

And two together go
Into the forest, with intent
To love and grow;
Branches embraced and bent—

Brave pattern for
World's tottering wall;
A roof of hands
Against sky fall.

Tale
for Malcolm Lowry

It was not the lock that disturbed—for I had the key
But over the lock, that web of filigree
And the large black witch who watched
From her wheel house, so intricately latched.

Some might have taken warning, gone away
Up sodden path, through evergreen
Past devil's club and spleen
Dashed into daylight and the hard highway

But I took the key, fitted it into lock
And turned. The spider house split loose,
Witch scuttled off to hide, fell prey
For the intruder's foot, the stranger's way.

So did I come to own that hen-legged house,
And the house, surprised, grew meeker than a
    mouse.

Malcolm, I wrote some poems here for you
Defying all black magic: hear me, hold me true.

Interval With Fire

Before I began to burn
with new found fire
this wintry summer had blown,
had flown over.

Before I made the discovery
staked the claim
and stood at the rock's end
crying a name,

stood arrested
on the alpine meadow
in amber light
flowing like honey—

before realization
of the total wonder
winter spoke
clouds massed in thunder.

I lifted my pack
turned to rock's shadow
closing my eyes
from the amber meadow.

Where storm swung down
to chasms again
I weighed my way
in the chill rain.

❖ ❖ ❖ ❖

Now in the valley
past fisted cedars
black bog, lecherous arms
of devil's club

safe over burnt-out ledges
knee deep in slash
(the whited sepulchres
of our devotion)

safe at the level of
hitch-hike settlements
overflow from
a city's coldness

where the old man broods
on his apple tree, bitten
brown with evil
by the moth's bulldozer

and the old woman gathers
sour blackberries
from a wet season,
a sodden September—

safe, but unsure
(back in the common place)
that there had ever been
an amazement

upon my eyes, a blast
of energy electrifying
my mind, a morning
when the heart blossomed—

(for the time of every day
is the time of misgiving:
in the habit of living
begins disbelief.)

So safe, but unsure
in the wet glitter of blessing
showered from a cherry-tree
shaken in September—

the sky turned
and the rain shoved over:
I felt an arresting hand
held on the shoulder.

Sun called and controlled me
his shadow shared me
I rose to the mountains
where fire is no stranger

His day is now mine,
an entering river
his blaze in my blood
flowing forever.

Invisible Sun

Life is a pure flame, and we live by an invisible sun
within us.
— Sir Thomas Browne

At the end of a day my hands hold heat;
Dipped in the fire of love, they burn
Like radiant isotopes, to illustrate
Where hours went: hot in the washing water

Then seeking cellar shadows, cool cupboards
Where light of day shines from jewelled jellies:
Or upstairs in empty sleeping places
Tucking the light into a white sheet.

Oh, my hands have sung, have swung from the
        sun's centre
To be the veins of warmth within a room:
To burn with the work done and the night to
        come—
Rounded in sleep, to shape an invisible sun.

Faces Of Emily
(1948-1953)

The Three Emily's*

These women crying in my head
Walk alone, uncomforted:
The Emily's, these three
Cry to be set free—
And others whom I will not name
Each different, each the same.

Yet they had liberty!
Their kingdom was the sky:
They batted clouds with easy hand,
Found a mountain for their stand;
From wandering lonely they could catch
The inner magic of a heath—
A lake their palette, any tree
Their brush could be.

And still they cry to me
As in reproach—
I, born to hear their inner storm
Of separate man in woman's form,
I yet possess another kingdom, barred
To them, these three, this Emily.
I move as mother in a frame,
My arteries
Flow the immemorial way
Towards the child, the man;
And only for brief span
Am I an Emily on mountain snows
And one of these.

And so the whole that I possess
Is still much less—
They move triumphant through my head:
I am the one
Uncomforted.

*Emily Bronte, Emily Dickinson and Emily Carr.

The Door

When the house snaps out its lights
Shrouds hallways in diagonal dark
And fire folds hands, sinks down to sleep
And drowsy child is set adrift;

When books are closed and doors are locked
O then, then only,
From the parched day a fugitive
I bow, drink deep the well of silence formed
Banish the blaze where doubt and indecision
Hold and halt; reach out for flowing waves
Of wall; open a shadow door—and lo!

I leap, I run—swiftly to meet myself.

The Husband

My guardian angel is a forbidden man.
Banned from the garden, he forbids
all others entry.
He wears no sword, but turned it long ago
into a pilgrim's ploughshare:
Presbyterian, he paints the earth more black
the heaven more radiant white
than my plain eyes perceive.

My landscape's technicolour: paradise,
the plummetings and plumes from colour's prism;
I, colour's prisoner, am gardened by love's green
dance the eternal daylight on a shaft of sun.
What do you guard then?   Adam? Or Quixote?
My freedom lies within.
O arbitrary gates and perilous walls!
Your bounden duty staggers out of bounds.

Letter at Midnight

Behave to me with love:
I am one so self-encircled
Only a thoroughbred could hurdle
These tough hedges.

And there are traps beyond
Set by the cunning of hated hand

And crags to clamber
Only a bold surefooted beast
Would venture.

Behave to me with love:
I am a country field, untamed
Restless for rider.

The Morning After

I cannot weep again, although the tears
Came easily before—
Life on the fringe of feeling—
Now hard sense builds me a solid door
Where I survey the morning.

Red poppies were uprooted in the night
Dishevelled silken bloom
Mud-spotted on the tiling
And every hope down-fallen in swift doom
And every dream divided.

But growing still goes on, persistence lives
In tug of a child's hand
In voicing his question—
Tears will not build again the house long planned
Nor man the bastion.

Godmother

Round, little mouth
That cannot suck
Enough love from the heart
To satisfy

Small, brittle fist
That cannot beat
The world down with a blow

Fine fettled head
That cannot nod
More helplessly
Than now—

I, the unwanted guest
Open the door
Infest the gaiety
With stricken tongues:
I take the floor.

O little, little life
My only gift can be
This blazing blade,
This knife's sharp constancy.

Easter

Painful the probing spring
pernicious for
those who refuse
growth, for fear.

And is there fear
in each incisive thrust
of white shoot from the dark
cold kingdom of the loam?
And in each awkward wing
weaned from a leafy home?

Or is the human young alone
the unaccepting one
afraid to face the sun
or green fires of the bone?

Collage

Windy Easters bellow out the mind
For quick manoeuvres, tacking to the shift
Of memory: the Sunday sheets, and church
—But somewhere in the woods, anemones
Shy in their mauve retirement—mourning flowers.
So we remember feathered greenery
Coming early and veiled; and country stretches
The rippled breathing of the earth blown bare
Warm for young hands to touch.

So the Easter organs and the funerals
The cluttered streets, corners that scratch and rub
Recede, like byways never travelled on—
Instead of sharper knife, the flash of day
A magnet to that bursting green—the blade
Of growth; and you stand stricken so
Child and awakened woman, priest
And sacrifice, sunlight and sun's recipient,
Alone, and yet in unison—
Palms upturned to light!

Ferry Trip

This lull between two lives
when the commuter leaves his lawn
his roses ripe for pride
his girl-child, blossom-eyed;
when he, waving, says farewell
to the amenities of habit—
precautionary measures to adjust
the clock, the radio, the bus
all in a curving line that leads
from news, crammed between cup and lip
to the burned bridges—the ferry slip:

This twenty-minute lapse
from being observed, watched, waited for
attended to and goaded on;
this pause
fountains the heart!   She springs again
who half-alive was towed from winding-sheet
and told to dress, prepare
for the swift plunge across the Bay
to office desk and neon stare.

Not this, O heart. Cinema city. Not this
crossword travel to unravel
or siren to unreel,
its animal sound a snarl
on the fog-stained air!
Not this unreal and photographic self
swinging a cane for friend
whom no friends recognize, who dives
from the candid camera shot
into the limbo of an office room.

No. Sit still and be
other than he.
The one who, boy-legged,
scaled the mountain yonder
caught salmon in the Capilano
cuddled his sister, quizzed his nurse,
made off with the family purse;
the one who holds in his shy hand
modelled in memory, a new land
shaped like a woman, with cool contour
but solid as rock and the rock's future.

He is the one who, here
between two lives
can let both disappear;
who drifts to the inner island where
beating upon the ear
not tinkling brass, but throbbing as a gong
sounds the abundant, overflowing song.

Children's Camp

Call it safety—
That cool island where
No headlines glare
No rumour of the world
Disturbs the ear;
Boys' arms and legs
Are fancy-free
To spin like catherine wheels
Through hours of play
Until, at night
With campfire at the throat
Their hearts sing out, sing out
They chant their way and float
To airy sleep.

Though gongs awaken
Summer is a season of high bells
Rung in the skies, and shaken
Through green leaves calling out a dance,
Sun's baton striking time:
So bells ring out all day!
But clock's invisible
And day moves into week
Unchained by calendar or season;
Hours need no rhyme
And summer needs no reason.

Call it safety
That island where
No motors hum
No planes drone
No bombs loom—
Here childhood is miraged,
Anchored in dream
A cordon against sound.

Call it safety, where
Under the tall star
And the cedar bough
A dream takes form.

Epithalamium for Susan

(Susan Allison, née Moir, who on her wedding night rode over
the Hope-Princeton Trail to become "the first white woman of
the Similkameen." Later the Allisons settled at Westbank on
Lake Okanagan.)

I

A name beats in my blood—
Similkameen!
River of cool caress
and sudden flood
over whose veins we rode
gay and rough-shod.

That was a bridal ride
into Similkameen
with Indian as guide
and lover by my side
over the Skagit bluff
September scorched
where mountains opened up
mirror on mirror
each a reflection of
the other's face—
message of love
from a further place.
We moved from frame to frame
into a land unmapped
and crying for a name;
our horses' hooves
beat a new alphabet
on mountainside and lake
calling out:
Skagit, Cedars, Cayuse Creek:
the trail was tried!

2

At night the tales I heard
from Yacum-Tecum and I-cow-mas-ket
around our campfire, stirred
from centuries lost
from caves of silence drawn—
of satyr, shuswap and of giants born
invisible, save to the Indian eye—
those fiery myths breathed life into the stones
and made the boulders move
(I dared to touch one, and let loose a cry:
I was burned through.)

3

So it was true, as you
long afterwards accused:
I did not give myself to you.
For on that wedding-night
I was a girl bound over to the hills,
my essence pierced with arrows of night air—
tang of sagebrush and the clear
perfume of pine.
No linen sheets for marriage-bed, but I
lay soft on "mountain feathers"—spruce,
mouth stained with huckleberry juice;
as epithalamium I heard
the deep drum's beat, the guttural song
sounding in my blood and bone:
the river pounding loud and long
calling me home—Similkameen!

From New Poems
(1953-1955)

Genii

At night, in the country of rain
With rain walking the house
Nailing the roof,

I dream of California, never seen:
Gold globes of oranges, lantern lemons
Grapefruit moving in slow moons,
Saucers of roundness
Catapulting colour.

In the country of rain
Of salal and rowan berry
Of bitter arbutus fruit;
In the landscape of cloud;

I summon up the roller-coasting south,
Shake the sun's lion paw!

Bartok and the Geranium

She lifts her green umbrellas
Towards the pane
Seeking her fill of sunlight
Or of rain;
Whatever falls
She has no commentary
Accepts, extends,
Blows out her furbelows,
Her bustling boughs;

And all the while he whirls
Explodes in space,
Never content with this small room:
Not even can he be
Confined to sky
But must speed high and higher still
From galaxy to galaxy,
Wrench from the stars their momentary notes
Steal music from the moon.

She's daylight
He is dark
She's heaven-held breath
He storms and crackles
Spits with hell's own spark.

Yet in this room, this moment now
These together breathe and be:
She, essence of serenity,
He in a mad intensity
Soars beyond sight
Then hurls, lost Lucifer,
From heaven's height.

And when he's done, he's out:
She leans a lip against the glass
And preens herself in light.

On Seeing

Far-fetched, the eye of childhood sees the whole,
Essentializes figures to the brief
Recording of a rounded head
And outlets for the senses —
Eyes, ears, astonished hands;
And then takes on at puberty
A pained perception of the detailed self—
An agonizing analyst with eyes
Shaped to the comic strips
And women puffed like robins for a worm.

The inward eye begins as infantile,
Sees only the broad outline of the self;
Until some blinding day
When stricken on Damascus way
The details are revealed:
Gnarled hands of age, distorted love,
The skin of sickness stretched upon a soul;
The look "I hate," the voice "I scorn"
The cry upon the deadly thorn:

This clarity is mercy for our sight:
Deformed, we seek the therapy of light.

Generation: 1955

I see them moving on the other shore
The young men, baffled, with no fruit in store
And winter coming on. They have not fished
Nor hunted; manna fell; they lapped it to their lips,
Made snowballs of the residue, and aimed
Their easy blow, like bear-cubs tamed,

Baring no cruel intent.

They're stranded now. The ice floes move
Inexorably toward their fading grove;
I see them herded on the farther ridge
Who never knew the meaning of a bridge:
Our signals flashed in code of human kind
They never learned; they see us, but are blind.
In vain our struggling tongues convey the news—
No use to battle, where we cannot bruise.

       The ice floes circumvent.

After Hiroshima

Not any more the visions and revelations
A voice at Emmaus, a figure of light on the hills;
Not any more the courtesan running early
To pray, and the prayer answered in act: an
      astonished tomb.

We see no mysteries; miracles are not accepted,
The beating rain bears no messages for man;
Though sun may still burn hot, searing the skin
No hearts dare listen while fear stirs the womb.

What the right hand doeth, stirring the pot of evil—
The hydrogen brew; the left knows not, is sleeping;
If the mind asserts, the heart dare not conjecture;
The picture upon the wall is unveiled, but dare not
      speak.

Not any more the visions and revelations:
Only in brief flashes is light received, good news.
Only a child's belief, rocked in a cradle of doubt,
Can prophesy our safety; illuminate our hope.

The Dark Runner

Around the circle of this light,
This self, I feel his nudging nerve,
His prying finger seeking the concealed
Small crack where my intent might swerve.

He's sensitive to softness; hurries out
The all-too-eager love; the willingness
To let a fault grow large in wilfulness
Until it swings a window upon doubt.

The integer is I; integral while
I'm centred in sun's round:
But O, how swift the door is swung
And fumbling darkness found.

This Arrow

This arrow strikes me with the force of light
As if sped from the sun and aimed by him
To burn me to the quick;
And though I walk the ordinary way
And none can see the shaft bi-secting me,
I am not whole; and shall not be again.
I am not whole, as flesh is known to be
But move divided; here, on earthy feet
There, flashed with heaven's heat.
O do not find me, do not seek to know
What shaft upholds and arms me from you so.

Winter Song

That shining, polished air
You breathe in your eyrie
Is mirror-clear,
Frost-fiery.

But your component's water
Murky, dark
Reflects the ominous
Sullen spark.

Clouds close over
Your cool covey
Sunshine marches
From your shadow

And deeper than flash
Of fin in well
Your thoughts dot, dash—
But never tell.

O when will you freeze
Glassy, clear
Frost-breathing image
On polished air?

Other

Men prefer an island
With its beginning ended:
Undertone of waves
Trees overbended.

Men prefer a road
Circling, shell-like
Convex and fossiled
Forever winding inward.

Men prefer a woman
Limpid in sunlight
Held as a shell
On a sheltering island...

Men prefer an island.

But I am mainland
O I range
From upper country to the inner core:
From sageland, brushland, marshland
To the sea's floor.

Show me an orchard where I have not slept,
A hollow where I have not wrapped
The sage about me, and above, the still
Stars clustering
Over the ponderosa pine, the cactus hill.

Tell me a time
I have not loved,
A mountain left unclimbed:
A prairie field
Where I have not furrowed my tongue,
Nourished it out of the mind's dark places;
Planted with tears unwept
And harvested as friends, as faces.

O find me a dead-end road
I have not trodden
A logging road that leads the heart away
Into the secret evergreen of cedar roots
Beyond sun's farthest ray—
Then, in a clearing's sudden dazzle,
There is no road; no end; no puzzle.

But do not show me!   For I know
The country I caress:
A place where none shall trespass
None possess:
A mainland mastered
From its inaccess.

❖ ❖ ❖ ❖

Men prefer an island.

Nocturne
for *Alan Crawley*

Countries are of the mind
and when you moved upon my land
your darkness ringed my light:
O landscape lovely, looped
with loping hills, wind-woven
landfall of love.

All my frozen years
snow drifting through bare birches
white-cowled cedar
and the black stream threading through ice—

All sultry summers run
barefooted through the crackling wood
flung upon rocks made skeleton
x-rayed by the raging sun—

All springs, wild crying with the wood's mauve bells
anemone, hepatica
breast against bark, the sap's ascent
burning the blood with bold green fire—

All autumns, solitary season
treading the leaves, treading the time:
autumns that stripped deception to the bone
and left me animal, alone—

All seasons were of light
stricken and blazing—
Only now the shout
of knowledge hurls, amazing:
O bind me with ropes of darkness,
blind me with your long night.

From Selected Poems
(1956)

Signature

LIVESAY THE NAME GOD THEM GAVE
AND NOW LIVES AYE INDEED THEY HAVE.
— Lines on an English tombstone

Born by a whim
This time
On a blowing plain
I am as wind
Playing high sky
With a name—
Winnipeg!

So prairie gave breath:
Child head, anemone
Raised from winter grass
Pushing the mauve-veined cup
Upward to world all sky
Peopled with cloud.

Ages before
These violet veins
Fingered their mauve
Through England's green;
These crocus eyes
Glowed in stone
Or a poplar row
Sturdy with Normandy;
Or a sea-wall—
War's peep-hole.

And longer than summers
Of conquering blood
Were my feet running
In a Roman wood
And my hair bound
In a vestal hood.

Stretched on the solitary sand
Of Egypt, I lay asunder:
Till the lover came,
The flowering night
Shaped me a name
And the earth shook under.

Now when I waken here,
Earthbound
Strapped to the sound
Of a Winnipeg wind;
I dream of the next step
On into time—
Casting off skin,
Bones, veins and eyes,
Flower without root,
Dancer without feet—
Gone in a cone of spiralled air,
And I only wind
Sucked to the sun's fire!

THE PRAIRIE GAVE BREATH; I GREW AND DIED:
ALIVE ON THIS AIR THESE LIVES ABIDE.

Of Neighbours

Let us love our own, our joining generation:
Not so much, our fathers and our sons.
These move half a world only
In our sphere, and run clear
From parapet and thicket this side of fear—
Jump, heaven hiding, to their goal
Ours not choosing, but their own fox-hole.

Who would go unburdened, sky-free, caring
Would be with his neighbour laughing and
        sharing:
But stubborn as hate, resistant as love
Comes one man to another equal and brother.

Chant

Harrow me, Lord,
Into a lively neatness:
The free, controlled release
Is featness.

My bolt into the world
Was of the whole cloth,
Shapeless, senseless;
O shear me to semblance
Of order, persistence!

Pattern me with caution
Cougar-fashion,
With cunning of black bear
Cuffing cub from snare.

Store in my heart's chamber
The honeyed amber:
And let my faring
Overall
Waterfall
Be salmon-daring.

Make me a tree-sailor:
Inveterate underground
But tied to sun's trailer,
Soaring through sound!

Hymn to Man

Praise him,
>   Two-beaded, darting ant
>   Building the hill
>   His foot may smash—
>>   Let him be praised.

Praise him,
>   Silver-armoured
>   Lean as a spear thrown
>   Salmon spirit
>   Caught in the hook of his cunning—
>>   Let him be praised.

Praise him,
>   High antlered and bounding deer
>   Rooted to earth when his gun booms
>>   Let him be praised.

And you,
>   From the snow pillow of perennial wings
>   White swan,
>   Praise him before the bullet's drawn
>   Its pencil, red on snow.

Praise him,
>   Pools of fir
>   And rivulets of cedar:
>   Who sucked your springs
>   With his hand of fire
>   Blacked out your boughs—
>>   O yield him praise.

And you, Sun, Galaxy,
    Holy and worshipped through milleniums,
        Stoop now and sing his praise
        Who caught your heel, Achilles, and then stole
        Your secret fire and ran with it
        Sowing the seams of cities till they burst:
        Explosion of small arms and legs
        Flowers of faces sundering the skies—

        Praise him!   Who holds your power now
        And steers with it
        Into a maddened ride:
        Life-splintering pride.

Praise him,
        All principalities and powers.
        His end is ours.

At Sechelt

Sea is our season; neither dark nor day,
Autumn nor spring, but this inconstancy
That yet is continent: This self-contained
Organic motion, our mind's ocean
Limitless as thought's range, yet restrained
To narrow beaches, promontories
Accepting her in silence; the land's ear
Forming a concave shell along the sands
To hear sea's shuffle as she leaps in gear
Spuming her poems upon our ribbèd hands
Crying against our poor timidity;
O come to bed in bedding water, be
Swept to these arms, this sleep, beloved and proud!
You'll need no linen; nor, thereafter, any shroud.

2

Now that I walk alone along the stones
I am compelled to cry, like the white gull
Light as snow on the undulating wave
Riding, lamenting. Though he lie
Forever feasting on the sea's blue breast
And I am shorebound, sucked to the hot sand
Crunching the mussels underfoot, scuttling the crabs
And seared by sun—still we are, each one,
The bird, the human, riding the world alone
Calling for lover who could share the song
Yet bow to the denial; laugh, or be mute;
Calling, and yet reluctant to forego
For otherness, the earth's warm silences
Or the loquacious solace of the sea.

Lament
for J.F.B.L.

What moved me, was the way your hand
Lay in my hand, not withering,
But warm, like a hand cooled in a stream
And purling still; or a bird caught in a snare
Wings folded stiff, eyes in a stare,
But still alive with the fear,
Heart hoarse with hope—
So your hand, your dead hand, my dear.

And the veins, still mounting as blue rivers,
Mounting towards the tentative finger-tips,
The delta where four seas come in—
Your fingers promontories into colourless air
Were rosy still—not chalk (like cliffs
You knew in boyhood, Isle of Wight):
But blushed with colour from the sun you sought
And muscular from garden toil;
Stained with the purple of an iris bloom,
Violas grown for a certain room;
Hands seeking faïence, filagree,
Chinese lacquer and ivory—
Brussels lace; and a walnut piece
Carved by a hand now phosphorus.

What moved me, was the way your hand
Held life, although the pulse was gone.
The hand that carpentered a children's chair,
Carved out a stair
Held leash upon a dog in strain
Gripped wheel, swung sail,
Flicked horse's rein
And then again
Moved kings and queens meticulous on a board,
Slashed out the cards, cut bread, and poured
A purring cup of tea;

The hand so neat and nimble
Could make a tennis partner tremble,
Write a resounding round
Of sonorous verbs and nouns—
Hand that would not strike a child, and yet
Could ring a bell and send a man to doom.

And now unmoving in this Spartan room
The hand still speaks:
After the brain was fogged
And the tight lips tighter shut,
After the shy appraising eyes
Relinquished fire for the sea's green gaze—
The hand still breathes, fastens its hold on life;
Demands the whole, establishes the strife.

What moved me, was the way your hand
Lay cool in mine, not withering;
As bird still breathes, and stream runs clear—
So your hand; your dead hand, my dear.

The Traveller

There he leaps, the tall young man!
I have often seen him on my travels.
Always breezy, always amazed,
He dare not stay long in one place.

On shipboard he lives a lifetime
In a week, exploring the souls
Of stewardesses or spinsters,
Young things yet unpetticoated;
Stirring in them
Longings for land, for four walls,
Four hands in a green garden.

But—foot on shore, he flies,
He's off after that Gothic steeple;
Goes boating under river bridges;
Adjudicates at an archery contest.
And the girls whose hearts he pried open
With his gentle, surgical hands—
Their secrets are tossed in his knapsack,
Their tears fall, not upon him,
But upon their own childhoods.
The fault, they say, lay not in him
But in their own roots.
"Why must I go alone?" he cries,
To each and every: "Come!"
But they bide at home.

Last spring I saw him soaring
In a crowd of coronation girls
All garlanded, entwinèd in their curls;
And when I looked again
The troubled air grew thin—
Without an explanation or good-bye
He made a cool connection with the wind,
Was never seen in these parts again.

Wedlock

Flesh binds us, makes us one
And yet in each alone
I hear the battle of the bone:
A thousand ancestors have won.

And we, so joined in flesh
Are prisoned yet
As soul alone must thresh
In body's net;

And our two souls so left
Achieve no unity:
We are each one bereft
And weeping inwardly.

The Skin of Time
for Alan Crawley

i

Across a generation
Caught
The eye exchanges truth
My skipping-rope comes out
My heart
Plays hopscotch with your youth.

What help is there, this side?
How can I cry to age:
Deepen my wrinkles,
Smooth out love's fierce rage?

How can I cry, when I
Feel timeless, ageless, high
As heaven's hemisphere?
How can I cease to live
Borne by your breath, my dear?

O ease me from this fever and this folly
Stop with a word the swirling carousel:
Shrill tune and shrieking images
Confuse me as I whirl.

And from this joy release me, from this high
Excitement kiting me through air:
The world kaleidoscoping falls away
As, fanned by you, I fly.

Break, break the guiding ropes, the taut
Intensity of thought to thought—
I cannot soar forever at your will,
Nor flutter down whenever you are still.

iii

The inner and the outer room
Of my lord's world I pace
There is no antidote to bliss
Within, unless a bliss outblown.

Ongoing, I outstretch the air
So high my greening grows
My hands are stems, my blood the life
Teeming along these boughs.

But inward, inward stem the storm
Spread fire on these walls:
The image of the waking wood
Sustains the body's fall.

iv

Though I be desperate, I dare
No tyranny of power
The democratic act
Is second nature now.

My first wild will is curbed
Not from commonsense:
Because a sea of hands around
Votes in my innocence.

I cannot choose the way
Of loving you alone:
The conclave of my memories
Keeps my allegiance home.

v

"Accept with grace" was ever the aim—
Consummation is otherwise:
To have a habitation and a name
And time to dust the dark behind the eyes.

You, aging, face your dark
Living to yesterday
Relinquishing the spark
Intent on keeping gay.

But I, midway between
That youth, that age
See in the wrinkle's seam
The stitch that shrouds me from
A wider room:

And still I hold
Persistent certainty
That leaping from world's rim, a boy,
Youth circumnavigating light
Would fire me to full joy.

Last spring he came; and I
Stood helpless by:
Masked in the skin of time,
The stuttering tongue of rhyme.

On Looking into Henry Moore

1

Sun, stun me, sustain me
Turn me to stone:
Stone, goad me and gall me
Urge me to run.

When I have found
Passivity in fire
And fire in stone
Female and male
I'll rise alone
Self-extending and self-known.

2

The message of the tree is this:
Aloneness is the only bliss

Self-adoration is not in it
(Narcissus tried, but could not win it)

Rather, to extend the root
Tombwards, be at home with death

But in the upper branches know
A green eternity of fire and snow.

3

The fire in the farthest hills
Is where I'd burn myself to bone:
Clad in the armour of the sun
I'd stand anew, alone

Take off this flesh, this hasty dress
Prepare my half-self for myself:
One unit, as a tree or stone
Woman in man, and man in womb.

Poems From Exile
(1958-1959)

The Voyage Out

I at ship's prow
wind-willed
splashed with spume
see where white pencil
hieroglyphs illume
green heaving marble:
away she ploughs
cleaving for elbow-room.

With your wild waves
flagging me down
(breath seized from lung,
wind talking on my tongue)
now hold me numb—
for on green glass
where foam-white pencil flies
flashes the face I mourn.

The Absences
to Duncan: January 1959

What days of disbelief
cut in this diamond, trust!
What lapses in our love—
yet love we must.

For us no future tense,
past tension's set:
the mould of other times
contains us yet.

But on these planes
we made mountains move:
our separation plots
the curve of love.

After Grief

Death halves us:
every loss
divides
our narrowness
and we are less.

But more:
each losing's an encore
of clapping hands
dreaming us on;
the same scene played once more
willing us grander than
we were:
no dwarf *menines*
but kings and queens.

And still, some say
death raises up
gathers the soul strong-limbed
above the common tide
to catch a glimpse
(over world's wailing wall)
of an exultant countryside.

Praise and Lament

The wind at Land's End tore the roots of air
The yellowed grass, the brown hummocks of war—
Barbed wire and cement still tangled there
Though men had gone. Wind was alone.
Sea writhed below, licking its wounds, rock-wrent.

The wind at Land's End on a day so bare
Of sun, engendered its own solitude,
Tore flesh from heart, revealed its lonely beat—
The drum of men sounding beneath earth's skin
To moss and stone not kin; unearthly, separate.

The wind at Land's End tore these words from me:
(Listened to and heard by none):
A cry against the dark? Or praise for light?
Wild messages in code unknown.

The Ring

I have two hands; one moves in upper air
Circling the sun. It makes the playboy stare
Hard at the sky, watching the sudden flare
Of signal smoke: what messages for man?

My other hand is strange, unknown
Its work is subterranean,
Lifts from the water a white flash
And then is gone.

I have two hands that bind.
To shift the weight of light
From summer's hand into the winter one—
Would this restore my sight?

Or must I endless climb
The ladder upward, wear a jewelled sun
Only to plunge down, down, on the turning tide
And hide my signet under a heavy stone?

Widow

No longer any man needs me
nor is the dark night of love
coupled

But the body is relentless, knows
its need
must satisfy itself without the seed
must shake in dreams, fly up the stairs
backwards.

In the open box in the attic
a head lies, set sideways.

This head from this body is severed.

This Wisdom

This wisdom tooth
is winter proof

Buried in the gum and bone
it holds its secret as a stone
half hidden under snow; or fish
loitering in coils of ice.
It weaves its song
soundless among the roots of spring.

The quivering soul
walking a bridge of glass
sees the black waters boil
and fears to fall—

But secretly the seed
upholds his rooted need.
This wisdom tooth
like iron, is splinter proof.

A Ballet of Squares

1. TRAFALGAR

Sunday afternoon:
November's rain.
Four lions yawn.
The Admiral looks down in stone.

Under umbrellas
huddled exservicemen
shelter their slogans:
NO MORE WAR

and at a command
move off, sheepish, towards Pall Mall
protected by six young policemen
and a wreath.

Sleek-backed dolphins in the fountain
spew air with water
and swallow again.
Doves puddle after.

2. NOVEMBER ELEVEN

In Soho Square
night's nailed to the door
festoons of crape
looping remembrance.

We lean, arm in arm,
upon iron railings—
black pool of park
irised with shadows.

In blundering darkness
voices still whistle,
shadowy caresses
fumble for friendship.

We hold hands: neither saying
but both believing
in a sea cliff, green downs, windhover
and two loves leaning over.

In Soho Square
night swoops, a cutthroat
slashing remembrance. . .
black ribbons flutter.

3. FITZROY

Carriages and tossing horses
manoeuvre round the oval garden
eighteenth century heart
of the Square's rectangle.
They draw up smartly
at far-framed doorways,
by fluted columns,
pause at the green door with the gnarled brass knocker,
champ for George Bernard Shaw.

But he does not open the door
HE DOES NOT DESCEND THE STAIR.

(In this raw autumn air
the houses resound with emptiness;
nailed to the doors are plaques of businesses,
brain-trusts and barristers
and manufacturers of underwear.)

Crash, carriages, collide!
And horses, rear!
their oval eyes
roll in the mad square.

4. EUSTON SQUARE: QUAKER MEETING

This pool of silence holds us in its arms—
a cradle rocked by wind.
The small sounds of the world
sift down and spin
through weaving leaves
and far above, serene
the untouchable sky
sends radiant fingers of light
to probe the water's depth.

The circle is complete: the faces bent
sounding the pool.
Only an old man stirs
too restlessly—
a tremour skims the air

We share his sigh.

5. RUSSELL SQUARE: WINTER

Bereft   no residue of word
to celebrate   be sung
empty the mouth that senses salt
doctoring the tongue

Winter invades   leans shadowless
on plane trees and stiff lawn
day's blue shoulders in the loom
of mist   are hunched   withdrawn

Even the hard-crunched ground
welcomes no lovers lost
heaves from its bristling hedge
a brittle train of frost—

How leap from these constraints
cold-shouldering me
insensate garden
stony   stubborn   tree

into that locked
encounter with the eye
handshake   that hauls
earth into hug of sky?

6. MOTHERING SUNDAY

On a park bench
rain-drizzled
tough old woman
in grizzled beret, thick black boots
sits smoking a cigarette
as if it were May Day!

Down the rock-bottomed street
a boy in shorts
sprints on thin white legs
bats football about
from iron railing into iron railing.
He is bone cold.

On the old man's barrow
mimosa, tossed fountains and rivulets
flow from the South's fold,
daffodils defy
limp yellow tulips
and the iris mourn, washed blue.

But what I buy—
memento of the mesmerizing sun—
is round
is marigold!

Wine from Cyprus
(during the struggles)

Golden this liquid of the sun
yellow as the blood of trees.
I bought, I drank, I felt the iron squeeze
a ring around my throat
and choke me to the knees.

And choking so, the wine
with murder in its mien
from unsuspecting vine
culled those green eyes of light
to stare at mine:

to stare at a boy's blood
running the orchard ditch:
the body pitched, the thud
tearing at twisted root
staining the ancient mud—

staining my body's bread
draining my golden veins!
I am the one who's bled:
and I the unturned stone
holding his head.

The Dismembered Poem

Because in a moment of thaw
the poem saw light
was nailed on a café wall
chanted at night

It is now required to recant
to recapture the words
flown out into air
faster than summer birds.

What matter if song be condemned
declared null and void
torn limb from limb
dismembered, destroyed?

The words like seeds exist
declare themselves in air
behind walls, on the hidden ear
under the crack of the door

Around a fire, in the gloom
sombre the faces gaze
then flare at the words flung out
from memory's blaze.

Recant! Recant! that cry
is only a public noise:
behind the door in the dark
affirms the exultant voice.

To Speak With Tongues
(1960-1964)

Pictures at an Exhibition
("United Nations")

i

Everywhere
grass is ringed
La pelouse est défendue.
But close to the Eiffel Tower
two Englishmen and a girl
can't read French:
their iron chairs loll in the sun
at the forbidden centre.

Even I dared, myself,
to sit at the root of a pine tree
in the Zen garden
surrendering to waterfalls
and water lilies—
but the *gardien* got me.
"You're not decorative!" he shouted:
"this garden is to look at
not to sit in."

ii

Frenchmen are so egotistical
(I told the young traveller)
They won't take the trouble to learn our language.
At any rate,
ask a question in English
and you'll get a French answer.

Si égocentriques
(began my hairdresser)
J'ai trouvé les anglais—
Why, even if you ask a question in French
they reply in English!

The art of indecision
is practised quite a lot.
In this game of noughts and crosses
the casual Asian cancels out
every European thought.

Naive newcomers
sometimes try
to be human here.

Once bitten,   though
twice shy.

The stenographers
are gossip's new invention.
Worse, they spy
on each other
and decry
each other's boss;
they smile and smile
sowing dissension.

They've never been known to lose.

Arrowcollar man
shining American
in gear for steering
and human engineering.

But do not tamper
with his temper
or prick his pomposity:
he's a bureau-
cat.

vii

Ghana man
goes cautious as a tiger
through the jungle of
United Nations.

viii

In the top-floor restaurant
we damn the bloody French
and yet they pull it off, no jokes:
forever finding life in art
and art in artichokes.

ix

I hear God's dancer on the roof:
some call it rain.
The tower totters
voices splinter off—
but tongues, amazed
sprout forth again.

Let's mix our alphabets
juggle our syntaxes
make angels into poppycocks
and peacocks plain:
in my new Arabic
God's dancer is for rain.

A Conversation

Poets feed on each other's garden.
Gazelles, they nibble over the wall
the green flavour of other trees
bluer hydrangeas, more dangerous suns.

Unscrupulous, they eye each other, certain
the other perceives his secret love,
wears the same dark diving bell
exploring undersea, while talking loud above.

Poets cannot be sailors
but go submarine
handling the coral as a connoisseur,
shaking the seaweed from a labyrinthine lair—
they know each other as a silver fin
salutes in the green gloom
its flashing, phosphorous kin.

Houdini Eliot

Houdini Eliot hoodwinked the age
set critics in a tortured rage
ignored *Yeats* singing in his tower,
Graves, erudite in sensuous bower.

Magician, necromancer, fraud
he sang of sex, but had no bawd;
sceptre and incense swang he wide
to drown the stench of man's mean tide.

High priest of pomp and poetry
his formulations fogged the issue
his incantations are revealed
as fabrications, shreds of tissue.

Reader, did he hold you fast?
Did words so conjured rope your soul?
Unshackle now; undo the ill
unmesh the muse, and see man whole.

Picasso, Sketching

He lays his lines, blaspheming rules' precision,
silver and black converging, juxtaposed,
angles colliding, parallels enclosed:
distorts perspective, daggers the bull's eye
and then, his cornucopia conjured from thin air
tossed to a corner, dazzles out a scrawl—
Hen's tracks? Hen's eggs? Hen's teeth? They purl
and plane; ripple and pearl to grey again.

Il faut risquer tout!
Smoke from a tunnel belches cumulus,
the rearing engine truckles to its tracks,
snorts to a pause; develops eyes and nose,
is Taurus-teased, insanely furious.
Busy the fingers fly to tame it down
seizing the rein and haltering the frown
then easing to its customary stance—
Et voilà, ça m'amuse!
Stationed but champing, belching fire and fuss.

So does he shunt his visions through the station,
sets dynamite in open air, ignites creation.

The Second Language (Suite)

ZAMBIAN WEDDING

Demure she sits
under the white veil:
never must eyes be lifted
nor lips move

Even after church
seated under the canopy
an outdoor queen
with the bridegroom beside her
and retainers at attention
she does not cast a glance
at the old uncle, haranguing
the bridegroom
warning him as he lays a bare knife
on the gift table.

Others bring pennies linked with
admonitions to the bride
and the mother-in-law
leads in a circle dance
around the tent.

O *Sevah*
Sevah become *Mulenga*
when night falls
will you make bold, then
to lift up your eyes?
Will you be afraid, in that stillness
to behold the bridegroom?

In the cathedral
built on the highest ground
at the bidding of the priest
(a beloved Italian)
In the cathedral unencumbered by benches
you knelt on the bare floor
and I stood behind you
not able to believe.

The altar was plain
and behind it a great painting soared
not a cross
but two black men, murdered:
the Uganda martyrs.
"Christ was a black man too"
the priest had said.

Incongruously: the aisles,
lit with lights held in their niches,
the stations of the cross
the virgin blue and gold
the pink-faced infant.

As we came out
from the cool pillars into pillared heat
I did not ask you how you accepted
the mediaeval saints, swathed in blue robes
alongside the stark, the naked black.
I did not ask where your faith began
and ended —
I but thanked you.
Serene, your eyes answered:
"I have been wanting and wanting
for you to see it."

Moving together, not touching
but moving together
we walked down the hill into the roaring compound.

On the village green
circled by huts
shaded by palm trees
a woman was speaking:
tall, gaunt, with flexing arms
she swayed like a dance
from one side of the crowd to the other
shouting in Bemba
the language cleaving and cutting the air
as her arms flayed.

A fluttering crowd of women
in kerchiefs and coloured shawls
baby weighted, shifted
listened:
men lolled on the sidelines
black trousers, white shirts.
They showed their teeth, mocking
or shouting approval.

—What does she say? I asked you:
   You listened, frowning.
—She says, if the men are cowards
   they fear authority
   they tremble in the face of the police
   she says:
   If the men will not act
   the women will!
   the women are fearless.

—And is she right, Raphael,
   is she right?

—I do not know, you said:
   I do not go with violence
   nor violent women.

—*It is easy to kill*
   you said—
   and led me away quickly.

THE SECOND LANGUAGE
for Raphael

i

We walk between words
as if they were trees
touching rough bark
exploring origins.
Linked, in this green shade
a tree's name shadows us
I share its history
with you
who came
a first man to this forest.
And you find roots
your look uncurls each leaf
till every word we speak
thrusts upwards from its mother dark
and sparks our eyes with light.

ii

Now in our black
forest
moonlight fructifies
leaves go silver:
soundless shadows,
the trees parade
star-pierced
in a blue light.

iii

How to examine heaven
how with naked eye
outstare fierce stars?
Our words are torn to shreds
by the shrill cicadas.
We turn away—
the wanting mouth
closed
the longing arms
clamped.

iv

If in the dark
I stumbled against your mouth
would my arms stay pinned
at my back—
            or shiver forward
                white flowering
                    into black?

v

And in between night's sheets
imagined conversations flower
more real
than day's   disjointed
sentences

And when lips seal
and sleep takes over
myth and irrelevance of dream
are drawn
a dark cover

vi

Then who shall blame the dagga smoker?
the madman who escapes in terror?
the drummer beating out his warning?
I also   also you
enter into league with these:
by you and me
(who do not dare to speak)
are such deeds done:
we suffer
and do not condone
we wait our turn.

From The Unquiet Bed
(1964-1967)

Without Benefit of Tape

The real poems are being written in outports
on backwoods farms
in passageways where pantries still exist
or where geraniums
nail light to the window
while out of the window boy in the flying field
is pulled to heaven on the keel of a kite.

Stories breed in the north:
men with snow in their mouths
trample and shake at the bit
kneading the woman down under blankets of snow
icing her breath, her eyes.

The living speech is shouted out
by men and women leaving railway lines
to trundle home, pack-sacked
just company for deer or bear—

    Hallooed
across the counter, in a corner store
it booms upon the river's shore:
on midnight roads where hikers flag you down
speech echoes from the canyon's wall
      resonant
      indubitable.

The Incendiary
for Duncan

Now that the poetry's bursting out
all over the place
firecrackers setting off explosions
under train wheels
bombs
under hydrants

"bloody marvellous"
I can hear you saying
your eyes bulging and blazing
with that flinty excitement

as if every bone in your body
though burnt now   to ashes
had started a conflagration
had gone off crackling
and shooting poems
all over the bloody map
Canada—

        country you came to, late
        and loved with hate
        and longed to set fire to

Soccer Game

O early let the ball
spin early O
and fall
through thin-spun misty air
right to the goalie's hug.

And bounce it once
hard to the ground
sharp, vicious kick
and beat
beat back again
into the sea of knees
the pounding field.

O let the ball be
lightsome, curl of light
tossed as a halo
head to head
knocked as a message knocks
between two men
who wheel and spin
manoeuvring
feet   head
          head   feet
but hands forever tied
unless "offside"
and on to sidelines
hugged to breast
round world, bounced
and then released.

And once again
into the melee, each
man tied to each
his shadow
dodging him
bogging and stopping him
round
round the field a dance
to the ball's bounce

      Until a sudden huddle
      waffles it
      between fast feet—
      the toe's a needle
        quivering
      towards the net—
      ball circles   soars
      and lunging
      it is plunged
      straight to the win

The crowd roars!
(but only the clock
has won).

Ballad of Me

Misbegotten
born clumsy
bursting feet first
then topsy turvy
falling downstairs:
the fear of
joy of
falling.

Butterfingers
father called it
throwing the ball
which catch as catch can
I couldn't.

Was it the eyes' fault
seeing the tennis net
in two places?
the ball flying, falling
space-time team-up?

What happened was:
the world, chuckling sideways
tossed me off
left me wildly
treading air
to catch up.

ii

Everyone expected guilt
even I—
the pain was this:
to feel nothing.

Guilt? for the abortionist
who added one more line
to his flat perspective
one more cloud of dust
to his bleary eye?

For the child's
'onlie begetter'
who wanted a daughter?
He'll make another.

For the child herself
the abortive dancer?

No. Not for her
no tears.
I held the moon in my belly
nine months' duration
then she burst forth
au outcry of poems.

iii

And what fantasies do you have?
asked the psychiatrist
when I was running away from my husband.
Fantasies? fantasies?
Why surely (I might have told him)
all this living
is just that
every day dazzled
gold coins falling
        through fingers.
So I emptied my purse for the doctor
See!   nothing in it
but wishes.
He sent me back home
to wash dishes.

iv

Returning further now
to childhood's *Woodlot*
I go incognito
in sandals, slacks
old sweater
and my dyed
hair

I go disarrayed
my fantasies
twist in my arms
ruffle my hair

I go wary
fearing to scare
the crow

No one remembers Dorothy
was ever here.

Roots

i

Second-hand city
        strangers call it
Vancouver   Vancouver
second-growth forest
        sirens and seagulls
second-hand stores
hand-me-down houses

but city where
        under the thumb-print of rain
love rages
city where
        Lowry walked
stumbling
        on the beaches.

                He lived in the west end once
                on Davie Street
                a house indifferent to strangers

                —But who can help her?
                he shouted on the telephone
                —who in this bloody city
                can take in a woman evicted
                and feed her children?

                He wanted to take us all
                        all
                and fold us in comfort
                of his huge bed
                but he stood by the window
                unable to move

                he shouted in the telephone.

In Stanley Park
the sea pounds
        on the beaches
poet pounds on poet's door
        and there's no answer.

Walk on the muddied tide-
line, son
I said—
gather shells
look, we will polish them
coloured for Christmas.
You hung them on green branches
brought the sea roaring
into the living-room.

Was it the dripping cloud
you suckled to
or cedar branches
seizing on your hair

springing new made
out of the frondy lair
tree house, tree cave
into high summer air?

Was it the mountain climbing
three boys camping out
fish in the lake
figures diving under?

Through winter afternoons
washed and swished with rain
I'd stand by the window
till you came running in:

"I never saw such rain
such darkness streaming down
I was born on the baked prairie
O son I miss the sun."

iii

Did you remember those beginnings
twenty years later
saying you'd drive me back
to my high land, dry land?

You with a son, yourself
in the warm womb started
took the time out
to map routes homeward.

iv

Hugging the *Fraser*
we sped higher and higher
you driving and I
        silent
until sun tore
the clouds apart
green sage-brush choked
the hillsides and our nostrils.
The car roared on
and yet we heard
high, clear
a cool sparkle of sound:
the meadow-lark.

Golden lies beyond
sun-fevered hills
greenland of lakes and rivers
mountain country
        (handsbreadth of green-
        gold fields
        in a split-second of sunlight).
We paused to drink in
the evening
and again
a meadow-lark marked us.

The mountains of *Field*
snow-draped
were chilling
the car swerved as
6 mountain sheep
catapulted the highway
Did you see him?
a timber-wolf chased them.
they stood   alert   tense
living antennae   and
possessed their safety:
the man-made pavement.

v

In Saskatchewan
they seem to hate trees
they hate the finger upraised
to disturb the flatness
not   *The Wind Our Enemy*—
but trees.

We drove and drove
dust devils swirled
black puffs of oil wells
choked
we drove in madness
yet eased   in the towns
to see one solid building
brick (a city hall?) pivotal
among false fronts

And after the shaken blackened houses
twisted on a ditchside
gaping doorways   aching silos
we were surprised, in *Saskatoon*
by a green welcome.

Whose wind?
What enemy?

Spring lilacs hung down, dusky
scenting the river.

vi

So we came to the border
(a buffalo on signposts)
the black soil rippled
not yet green-pricked.
We stopped by the roadside
so we could run down amongst last year's stubble
to stoop, to discover
the furry and furtive
mauve crocuses:
a keen wind blowing
air so fresh we grasped it
in lungfuls, armfuls.

vii

In the brown-shingled house
(brand new in 1911)
battered by *Winnipeg* wind
he is the last, shrivelled, small-limbed
member of the family.
He hugs close the past
in photographs skew-gee
studding the walls—
his scrubbing brush worn to the quick
snuffs at the same linoleum
(World War I)
his pantry a mouse-nest
of fluff, nasturtium seeds, bent forks
a box of corks
all sizes, any bottle.

Only outdoors
tending his seedlings
in the black earth, May-awakened,
only setting out tomato plants
and Grannie's geraniums
(generations of fire)
only as he looks up suddenly
beyond us, out into sky
his blue eyes
    terrify.

viii

I walk beside you down the oak-lined street
to the orange house, pitched roof
where I was delivered
and grew in darkness

overhanging eaves
snow-burdened
in summer the oak-leaves
sombre, olive
the garden a deep
mysterious tangle
poppies up to my shoulders
sweet-peas arching

in spring my father
poured the round seeds
into my hand—crusty and crooked.
Now!   plunge finger in, and dig
a narrow hole, just finger deep
release your hold
bury the seed.

I followed awkwardly.
and when the orange bells
musk-scented
burst into air
I lay down in the nasturtium bed
sucked at the burning leaves

forgot the digging
and the coarse manure
never connected that wild birth
orange and bleeding
with black soil, ignorant
and sleeping.

I walk beside you where I grew
amongst the flowers
and retain
in the scent of the sweet-pea
my mother's scissors, snipping
in the musk of nasturtium
my father's thumbs, pressing

    heart planted then
    and never transplanted.

Spring

The old girl draws a line upon the board
    and then another, so
and children creak, knees in a tension
like their finger-joints:
    they long to go
leaping the aisles of surreptitious eyes
into a gallop where the windows grow
    a long green land of love.

Winter was different.
The geometric lines
    white chalk on black
seemed relevant as snow
    outlining a bare tree.
She held them   with the chalk
    in her stiff hand
and wound them with her wand
into a maze of symbol
    drift of sound.

But now the thin line quivers
        in that room
a greenness sifts the heady air
eyes leap   the branch bursts into bloom
colour invades   the perpendicular.

Isolate

To find direction
the only child creates a web of action

pulling them in, to play
new, unknown games
making herself a centre

And everyday
she thinks of a new way
for charming them: some twist
to *Hide and Seek* they'd never thought of
some long manoeuvre of the map
of *Hoist Your Sails*.
And finishes, on Saturdays
holding them all intent
in half-pint chairs on the dish-towel lawn
chalking sums on a child's blackboard.

Then thunder breaks:
across the street
the firebell clangs
and the great grey horses stamp
in a burst of doors
deafen the asphalt with their hooves.
Games fall apart
as children fly like sparks
with whoops and shouts into the charging street.

She stands alone at the gate:
games fall apart.

Perceptions

Shrinking eyes   the child draws,
noting:
watch them shrink.

And he had watched
adult eyes
staring wider and wider
    then closing
        snapped shut
            refusing light.

Look! the child cries:
how can you stop looking?

The Emperor's Circus
(on seeing his drawings reproduced)

for Alden Nowlan

They called him cold   recalcitrant
old   in a dying court
he put
duty before grace
was to himself
unmerciful
        Franz Josef
imperator   impersonal

        Only a name:
        once it was plain Franz
        and he fifteen,
        learning now to dance
        taken by tutor to
        the Cirque français
        to see the acrobats
        watch horses prance.

Pulling his pencil out
his laughter caught the tumbler's leap
the circus master, elegant with whip
the acrobats half taken by surprise
mastering the air
and centred on each page
he drew the horses, tossing manes
the tremor of their hoofs, the cries
of innocent creatures circling the dust:
he saw the silence
yielding in their eyes.

Alone upon an empty throne
the old man frowned:
setting his house to rights
his papers in their proper place
he saw mild horses leaping
in that land once captured by his lines—
and could not bring himself
to rip the pages, feed the flames

but tossed them into time.

For Abe Klein: Poet

and lives alone, and in his secret shines
like phosphorous. At the bottom of the sea.
                                        A.M.K.

Drowned? Were you the one
drowned
or do I dream again
and do I hold your hand across a table
in a Chinese restaurant
Leo and Art gesticulating chopsticks?
Hand reaching to affirm
against the goyish laughter?

A drowned man now. . . Your hand
that delicate instrument
long servant to
the fervent ferment of thought
your hand lies twitching out
a spider's mark
on the bare table

And in the hive, your head
the golden bowl
bees buzz and bumble
fumble for honey amidst empty cells
where the slain poems
wingless, tremble.

ii

Break down the twigs, break down the boughs
But break not, Lord, the golden bowl.
                                    A.M.K.

My body is tree
my reaching boughs and twigs
are skeleton
meant to be
broken by stone
by shouldering snow
splintered by rain
cracked by the fingering frost

My body is given, Lord
to show Thy ways
I read where my roots go
assess the green
count leaves' ascension
into heaven's blaze

This will I willingly
submit to Thee:
my skeleton,
my tree.

iii

He breaks the wineglass underneath his heel.
A.M.K.

When they come
as they will come
the marching men
with kaftan and phylactery
mounting the stairs

And when your ears
hear for the last time
those long Kaddish prayers

(You lying in bed
in the next room
lone)

Pray
not with those Hebrew words
pray the winged praise he made
in English
on your wedding night
Singing the bride and all the seven days.

iv

The wrath of people is like foam and lather
Risen against us. Wherefore, Lord, and why?
A.M.K.

Tender the boy's song
and honey sweet
the Kantor's hymn
(Loud the descending beast
devouring them)

Fair, in the circling light
the 'green inventory'
of field and wood
the mother shielding
her in-yearning
outward-yielding brood.

But dark in the river's bed
the coiled sequestered shape
reared up, and spewed
his lava black
lather of hate.

Making the Poem
for Jack Spicer,
before his death

i

Dreams are just
                    furniture
Jack said
Like words you keep pushing around
till they fit into the room
                    somehow
I begin
        at the beginning

ii

Dreams are
                personalities
the eight sides of your head
shifting in sunlight
but dreams do not reveal
        they obscure

iii

The serial poem is a
                    progression
not a repetition
a movement
                breaking through
                                outwards
splashing the shore
the swimmer heaves himself upwards
onto a rock
                far from the highway

iv

I wake:
it's middle of night, danger
is the poem. Here
it's been waiting, counting, am I
ready?

v

                Terror
terror at the white line
            strain
never to finish
                        (don't let me finish)
there are
an infinitude   of   finishes
miracles
are a way out

vi

Sleep is the cave of the self
infants sleep
Narcissus
       in the cave of mirrors
                    sleeps
the old
wake early
dream
    rarely
the dawn birds make
a thankful music

Postscript
for Phyllis Webb

There was a man here, this morning
From Mars, looking us over.
—Why do you stay?
he said.
And I was at pains to set it
down
and ask myself

    Why not go?

    Walk along the wave-bent shore
    wind-twisted roots
    and as the tide and I
    measure our distances
    stalk out, barefoot
    a shrunken, bowed and heavy-bellied form
    skirt hugging the knees
    into the cold salt seeking my warm blood?

    Why not go?

The trouble is, it comes soon enough,
I told him:
we, down here, are constantly aware
that the moment lies lurking
between one drink and another
one shout and another
one kiss   one blow
and a heart's beat.

So why care?

—But I don't see why, he began.
You mean, what's the sense in waiting?
He nodded, all frightening fascination
his eyes tearing mine from their sockets.
So I had to find it
to dig frantic the pocket of memory
pull out all the irrelevances
and lay them on the table.

—What's this?   he cried, seizing
a handful of hair.
—A girl's first golden sowing
cropped at two years old —
softer than down
but gone now!   coarse hair, black
so wiry you'd never know.
It's the softness, I said, the gold—
is why.

And a marble: hard,
a world half-sea, half-sun
red at the rim.
—What's that to you?   he said.
—A boy's game, I cried
playing with the world
under a cherry-tree
under the moon's tide.
For a marble eye
I'd stay.

Then he found the bowl of a pipe
pock-marked with tobacco
smelling of human breath
dead fires.
—You care for this?
—It was his view of mountains:
he puffed them into his pipe
and out again.
Now I can recognize
mountains.

Anything else?
No. Not unless—
unless counting counts.
A cat can count her kittens
up to five.
After that
she's lost.
I count the man
the boy, the girl
and myself—
—and last?
—I count my verse.

That's counted you out, he said.

Woman Waylaid
for "Jim" Watts Lawson

Having to have
heat
for the cool evenings
by the lake

is having   to search
allmornings paths
stumbling   on antsnests
interrupting   traffic
for five newborn
blue butterflies
discovering   violets
the pale   open-to-sky
kind   no scent
meeting   head-on
the lion-headed
dandyman

having to have
heat
return empty-
handed
to face
pot-bellied stove
its greed:

it gapes
for leaf for twig for bark for tree
and cannot be fed

       on flowers.

Empress

The hornets are alive, anyway
nothing has daunted their determination
to pursue colour
                        and devour scent
(even the mundane scent
                        of country kitchen)

In an orange blouse, gold slacks
I sit in my doorway:
I am a banquet
bussed   huzzahed!

Sunfast

                        i

I lurch
            into the sun
fasten on green
            leaves dripping
                        in golden butter
I break
            fast
            munch morning

                        ii

If you want to tell me anything
shout it out loud
into the sun's mouth

he grins and combs
our underworld
with his golden teeth

Lawnmower's purr
    caressing grass
in my next-door- neighbour's
    garden
probes me
as if I stroked
cat's fur
played with
green claws

I am one
with rolling animal life
    legs in air
green blades scissoring
    the sun.

Pear Tree

Lucky this pear tree has no ears
can grow and glow in whiteness
        sunlightness
all undisturbed
      by snarling horns
        unmuffled hooting cars
          machine-powered lawn-
          mower pushers
        and machine-
          saws shrieking into wood

Lucky this pear tree hears
      if anything
small bird cries percolating
      through downwhite foam
and children chugging on the chains
         of sound
practising language

Lucky this pear tree seeped in sun
shivering the air
        in her white
                doldrums
taps with her roots
        the worms' kingdom.

Process

We take in meat, fruit
from the outside
to keep life going
and air, from the first
we take in to breathe

The startled light
makes orioles
where our heads loll
we shake from our feet
the pious dust
sparrows inhabit

We stare, with eyes
stone blind
at the pear tree where
the robin lilts
his convoluting
song

We let the cat
arch in her deadly leap
and the robin's gone.

In the long grass
glassy, we listen:
his feathers stiffen.

The Rat

Every night I talked to him
(but he paid no attention)
—Go away
leave me alone
I want to sleep
sometimes I even said please

When this didn't work
I tried tantrums
banging and screaming I hurled myself
into his corner
he would be quiet for a small while
alert, listening
but as I was falling asleep
he would start all over again
gnawing and cracking his jaws
demolishing barriers

In the end I had no reserves left
save one—
yes, poison

Not actually POISON
the label said
just a merciful
leukemia
a gasp of air at the end
a mad dash for water...

I found him, two days afterwards
he hadn't quite reached the lake
unslaked

and he wasn't a rat   but
a squirrel.

Flower Music

Cyclamen

All the day's light
in one butterfly
    white
the last on the stem

Geranium

Suddenly, out of gloom
underneath the hanging
scrotum cluster
    red buds bursting
to blaze the room

Peony

My neighbour's peonies
blow white
    with spilt blood
        at the centre
fragrant
    inviolate

What spite: the flowers
I have grown   tyrannically
that never blossom
       he fathers forth
so light
    so silken

Eve

Beside the highway
at the motel door
        it roots
the last survivor of a pioneer
        orchard
miraculously   still
        bearing.

A thud   another apple falls
        I stoop   and O
that scent, gnarled, ciderish
        with sun in it
that woody pulp
        for teeth and tongue
        to bite and curl around
that spurting juice
        earth-sweet!

In fifty seconds, fifty summers sweep
        and shake me—
I am alive!   can stand
        up still
hoarding this apple
        in my hand.

Second Coming

What unwithering
                is this?
        the gnarled tree un-
                knotting itself?
White in autumn
                the dogwood blossoms—
against red rowan
                is green and white
                coming   be
                        coming.

The Unquiet Bed

The woman I am
is not what you see
I'm not just bones
and crockery

the woman I am
knew love and hate
hating the chains
that parents make

longing that love
might set men free
yet hold them fast
in loyalty

the woman I am
is not what you see
move over love
make room for me

Four Songs

i

People will say
    I did it for delight
    you—for compassion

But long before
our bodies met
the bargain was
established, set

Give me the will, you said
and in return
take from my fill
of passion

    You did it from design
    I—from compulsion

       ii

It is the fire you love
not me   not both
burning my body
it envelops you
attracts the moth
and the murderer too

    Dido knew
    this fire
    and chose
    that funeral

       iii

And yet you knew
    my hunger

    the body blunt
    needing the knife
    the forked light-
    ning of tongues

    your blow
    eased me so
    I lay   quiet
    longer

But thirst remains
    thirst for cool
    cool water
    the gesture of your hands'
    white fountains

iv

I drink now
no fiery stuff
burning the mouth
I drink the liquid flow ⌣
of words   and taste
song in the mouth

The Dream

I met a unicorn; one seldom seen
in this dark wood;
each hoofprint set the turf ablaze
each eye held clustered dew;
and when he walked beside me, nudging his
cool nostril on my shoulder
such wind blew
as tore the hair out of my head
my eyes from seeing and
my breath from speech.
Then I dissolved, my body writhed
and sank down in the ground
only my small white breasts arose
ponderous and round.

I met a unicorn and bear his mark
his horn, his stabbing glance:
eyes pierced by that confounding light
move in a meditative dance.
I met a unicorn in that dark wood:
and strangeness blazed my blood.

Old Song

What you will learn
        is this
you cannot hold
        what vanishes

my arching brow
        mouth's bliss
are temporary
        as leaf, grass

your bones may melt
        in me
or in another woman
the essence is
        to catch the bird in season

hold, hold a snowdrop
        capped and cool
in the cold snow—
then let it go.

A Book of Charms

Wear this, you said
and gave me a rose
to press against my breast

at night I carried it
into my single bed
rose red it glowed

and as I slept its shape
scattered, its petals were
strewn on the white sheets

perfumed, I lay
between the leaves
love's book, and dreamed

you came and found me there
untangled me from petals and from sleep
read me in rosy light.

The Taming

Be woman. You did say me, be
woman.   I did not know
the measure of the words

       until a black man
       as I prepared him chicken
       made me listen:
       —No, dammit.
       Not so much salt.
       Do what I say, woman:
       just that
       and nothing more.

Be woman. I did not know
the measure of the words
until that night
when you denied me darkness,
even the right
to turn in my own light.

Do as I say, I heard you faintly
over me fainting:
be woman.

The Touching

i

Caress me
shelter me now
                from the shiver
of dawn
'the coldest hour'

pierce me again
                gently
so the penis completing
                me
rests in the opening
                throbs
and its steady pulse
                down there
is my second heart
                beating

ii

Light nips the darkness
                a white frost
breaking in ripples
                on a dark ground
like light your kisses hover
                touching my nipples
under the cover

iii

Each time you come
            to touch   caress
me
            I'm born again
                        deaf   dumb
each time
            I whirl
                        part of some mystery
I did not make or earn
that seizes me
                        each time
I drown
            in your identity
I am not I
            but root
                        shell
                                    fire
each time you come
I tear through the womb's room
            give birth
and yet   alone
            deep in the dark
            earth
I am the one   wrestling
the element re-born.

A Letter

Have begun
to walk with pride
with you, a tree
growing inside

Head in air
have got taller
as my past
shrinks smaller

The Vigil

I lay all night
and you not with me
but you came beside me
from the dream's distance.

When you saw my wound
the left hand bleeding
See, in a key place!
you came and staunched it.

I lay all night
lonely sleeping
you stayed, not far
watch keeping.

And Give Us Our Trespasses

i

Sometimes the room shakes
as the bed did shake
under love

sometimes
there's this
        quaking

ii

As if at midnight
a socket
was plunged in the wall

and my eyes sprang open

iii

Whenever I spoke
        out of turn, was it?
you'd press your fingers
        against my mouth:
        Listen.

I heard only your heartbeat

iv

My tongue
        was too long
my kiss
        too short
Inadequate I shrank
        from perfection

v

Yet charged
your beauty charged me

the receptor trembles

quivering water
        under the smite
           of sunlight

vi

The telephone
        hangs on the wall
always available
        for transmitting messages:

Why is it
        to lift the receiver
is to push the weight
        of a mountain?

vii

Between the impulse to speak
        and the speaking
        storms crackle

Forgive us our

    distances

The Notations of Love

i

You left me nothing, when
you bared me to the light
gently took off all my skin
undressed me to the bone

you left me nothing, yet
softly I melted down
into the earthy green
grass grew between my thighs

and when a flower shot
out of my unclenched teeth
you left me nothing but
a tongue to say it with.

ii

in my mouth
no love ?
only cruelty   you say

take love   take love
is my reply
the hard way

twisted and sparse
to find   facing the rock
the fountain's force.

iii

Crow's feet your finger follows
circling my eyes
and on the forehead's field
a skeleton of leaves

Only the lips stay fresh
only the tongue
unsheathes its secret skin
and bolts
the lightning in.

iv

I used to think
that Siamese twins
occurred only
in Siam
once disabused
I find their trace
no matter where
I am

especially around
these absences
our minds are twins
they circle and unite
my left arm is your right arm
bound   even in flight

v

My legs stretched two ways   disparate
until you came
and joined them
(lying down between)
now, even when we separate
my legs coil close
and feet unite:
they form a pedestal
whereon I turn, in sleep
circling, serene—
no longer desperate.

vi

I was naked
and you clothed
me

so, in the dead
of night
you whisper-
ed
no other word
      of praise
you found, in day
bright light
to say

but day or night, I
am undressed

dance
differently.

Moving Out

Dismantling our house
the features of our love are gone
our feet grow loud
in a bare room
arms long to lean
in softness between sheets
but all the paraphernalia and props
are out of reach

I can only stretch
for your arms now
and find an upright bed
between your bones—
without the body of your house
I'd have no home.

Poet and Critic
for Raymond Souster

i

Words are so much more
than the thing seen, touched
(I argue with you)
they caress the jar
colour its round belly
curl fingers round
its throat:
before the jar is tipped
words have us drinking from it.

ii

Your poems sit
small gods upon my shelf
saying (you say)
only as much as form and shape
can shout:
but what I bring to them
is outside, stranger
than that spelled message
and what I seal
on the poem's mouth
is my tongue's pressure.

Zambia
Initiation

From the twentieth of November
at the turn of the moon's tide
I entered the dark continent—
it was blazing with light.

In Lusaka the streets glittered as yellow glass
buildings rose, pure columns of spray
trees tossed on the skyline, violet
(inviolate jacarandas)
trees blazed in the parkway, firelit
(flaming flamboyants)
black men sauntering the streets
clothed in white
lifted their faces, polished, to the sun
wind stippled the fountains.

From the twentieth of November
I entered the resplendent sunlight
took shelter under trees
gold-fisted.

Village

Nameless, the village
the clay huts, the shorn grass roof
brown to the ground
nameless
the woman huddled beside a pale flame
and the child, bringing stools to sit upon
is nameless, boy or girl.

They do not love this place, or name it
they are too much of it
they smell of grass, of leaves
of the pitiless dust
they rise up with the rain
and die with it.

Between the land and themselves
they feel no difference
loving the earth no more
than a man loves his own hand:

Use it, and live
or cut it off, and die.

Wedding

At the periphery and fringe
of villages where drumming swings
the hand that does the drumming
moves the world
meets sun halfway
and hauls him over the rim

The hand that does the drumming
drums man home
to womb and woman
beats that rhythm
on black curving thighs
thrusts love upwards.

Funeral

Not the women waiting
sitting in groups, wailing
in hysterical fixed pitch

not the men standing aloof
correctly silent

not sultry dust
yellow-brown, borne
wayward by wind
round the house
hither and thither
round the thatched house
where the boy ran

not the long walk
in twos, in threes
through the village compound
wailing, wailing high
into the trees—
the grasses
touch, unbending
shoulder high from the rains

not slogging through black mud
along the pathway
pressing, pressing against the grasses
where the boy is carried
shoulder high:

But the box
unpainted
wrapped in black cotton
the box, the men plodding ahead with it
through unbroken stretches
pushing aside grass with their shoulders
to the pit where the men are still digging
as the hymn, faltering, rises
and is chained to air.

During the singing, no wailing
a heave, a strain of muscles,
thud: words intoned

Not these, but the box
lowered
and broken into, sundered
by that   cry!
child's scream
small brother's mouth
a great O open

            (arms, shawls
            wrap him
            pull from pit
            mothering)

Not the waiting
not the wailing
            spades scraping
            earth shovelled over the box

but the brother alone at the drowning
the brother killed with his cry.

The Leader

i

The Copperbelt night is a snake
strangling the drums
squeezing the air
from throats, from lungs
under its arching coils
a child's cry shrills
in the beerhall's roar
a cauldron boils

But the Copperbelt day is saved
by a strike of thunder
the man on the anthill
crying out *Kwatcha!*
wilder than rain pelt
or the beat of sunlight
children shout freedom
waving green branches.

ii

Heaven lets down a rope
whereon I swing
the clapper of a bell
on sounding sky

and all below
they cluster with uplifted faces
black on white
and sway like flowers
to my wild clanging

whether sun burns me
or moon rivets with steely eye
I shall ring on
till flowers are black mouths
and the stones bleed my song.

The Prophetess
(Alice Lenchina of the *Lumpa* sect)

When the rains began
trees shuddered and were green
the earth heaved
fingers of grass pierced the crust
lilies exploded, anemones
blew into being
out in the fields mushrooms
swelled
as women, belly-swollen.

You were with child then, Regina*
and like the others
set out to gather mushrooms
when the hard hills had lowered heads
to graze
when the wild fig trees offered shade.

Walking slowly, surely,
eyes to earth
sensitive only
to the earth
you moved off the path
circled round hills
into green shadow
umbrella trees:
          no one saw you.

        No one saw you.
        No one knew what had happened.
        Mulenga, your husband, wondered:
        he reported you "lost" to the Boma
        but no one went searching.

*Regina is pronounced *Lenchina* by the Bemba tribe.
 The mushrooms were of the type that induce visions.

One day
two days
three—was it three days?
on that day the women returning from hoeing
saw you walking through the gardens
towards the village.

> *Mulenga! Mulenga!*
> *Our sister is back, Lenchina!*

At first you sat silent, rapt
the child ripe within you
stirring
you sat on the ground, beside
a small flame
stirring the millet.

> *Call the elders,* you said.

And Mulenga brought them
to sit in the circle
to hear you speak:

> *Before you, my people*
> *I come as one naked, buried.*
> *For I who am living before you*
> *was dead*
> *and I who died once*
> *died three times.*

> *Pulled from the well of darkness*
> *by the words clanging*
> *clanging in my head*
> *I reached for the rim of light*
> *only to totter*
> *and fall again*

> *But again I was drawn*
> *pulled by the hair*
> *up into grey*
> *half-morning:*

and how I struggled
to hold on fast,
to listen, to stare
till the waters fell away
and I was hauled out safe
into dry air.

Look at me, look at me!
I am as one naked, buried,
for I who am living now
was dead, three times.

Ai   Ai   the people answered
cried out and marvelled
moved closer.

Not a white man's God I saw
lifting me up from death,
each time,
not a white man hammered with nails
on a wooden cross:
but a Lord incredibly shining
a sheath of light
and my eyes trembled at the brightness
when I heard a voice crying:

Lenchina, Lenchina, you cannot die
your time is not yet come
there is work to do

And he pressed a Book against my forehead
and showed me the songs I must sing
to rouse you, my people.

Ai   Ai   How the people cry out now
as the fire flickers
as the night falls sudden and definite
darkening the faces.
Not by a white man's God
need we be saved
but by the resurrection of a woman
an African mother
Ai   Ai

The drums beat
tentative   questioning
the drums come out of hiding
now strong ones   bold ones
the drums beat louder and louder
for you, Lenchina
standing by the fire now
short and stumpy
rooted as a tree
a tree singing the new hosannah!

Lumpa   (in the highest)

lumpa   the drums beat
lumpa   lumpa
lumpa   lumpa   lumpa

From Plainsongs
(1968-1971)

At Dawn

The going
and the coming of our love
holds me
in bed   unable
to move over from
your folded bones

Awake   I hear
the ferment
of your dreams
churning my pillow
as your arm swings
presses its light lever
gently upon my heart—

You turn
returning

and over all
my body's fingertips
day breaks
a thousand crystals

The Cave

i

I am the quivering needle to your north
the trembling arrow sped—
I never believed it
never thought me bound
until one night all night I lay
under your will and mind
and heard you play my secrets
over and over in your hand.

Taking my body so
on the unquiet bed
you pretend no care
save the act done, said

pretend you do not come
save for self-seeking ease—
take me or leave me there
just as you please

only when you sleep
coiled within that cave
your dream awakes me and your voice:
O love, we hold, we have.

The Woman

i

Don't hurry, I might say
when you first enter in
but then the urge takes hold
and it is I who cry
O hasten, quick untie
the fearful knot of pain
O hurry hurry on
and down
break me again
(until the bliss begins)

ii

When you make me come
it is the breaking of a shell
a shattering birth

how many thousand children
we have conceived!

Sorcery

My breasts are withered gourds
my skin all over   stiffens
shrinks—the pubic hair
bristles to an itch

Not to be touched and swept
by your arm's force
gives me the ague
turns me into witch

O engineer of spring!
magic   magic me
out of insanity
from scarecrow into girl again
then dance me   toss me
catch!

Dream

Sudden
a sceptred bird
swept through the window
into the blue room
and dazzled me

I swam in light—
he stooped
and pecked out my eyes
     I move in darkness now
     fumbling the walls
     trying to remember
     blue

          (I have closed the window
          and the sun falls cold
          through glass)

Auguries

Night shunts me on the rails of dark
into its own persistent
wayside stations

if I am to be married
I turn   in a blue dress
robin's egg
I turn in the heel of your hand
am grown younger
long hair blowing
an oval   a shell in your hand
to be broken

But night shifts me
to a dark situation
tree shrouded:
I feel their mop heads nodding
black arms pulsing
I am alone in a garden
with trees yelling

you have said no.

       Is there a green place
       further ahead
       a morning station
       where steel rails leap
       into sunrise?
       where blazing   I yet mourn
       the turns of the river—
       remember how my limbs rose
       and fell   under your loving
       how my breasts pushed upward
       as islands   out of water
       how your hands were the sky itself
       cupping my body?

       Is there a green place
       where you'll return again
       to lift me
       on girders of sunlight?

The Uninvited

Always a third one's there
where any two are walking out
along a river-bank   so mirror-still
sheathed in sheets
of sky   pillows of cloud—
their footprints crunch the hardening earth
their eyes delight in trees   stripped clean
winter-prepared
with only the rose-hips red
and the plump fingers of sumach

And always between the two
(scuffing the leaves, laughing
and fingers locked)
goes a third lover   his or hers
who walked this way with one or other   once
flung back the head   snapped branches of dark pine
in armfuls   before snowfall

      I walk beside you
      trace
      a shadow's shade
      skating on silver
      hear
      another voice
      singing under ice

Con Sequences

i

When the beloved
denies his body
my desire dies
also

ii

I look up
his face is stone
carved bone
unscarred yet
smoothed down

I wait for lightning
an avalanche
to tear the hillside

iii

Butterfly wings
clipped between two fingers
continue pulsing

iv

Step lightly
there is no assent
downwards

v

Kick the leaves
aside
yellow roots
cry for greening

vi

The sun shines
on the bald hill
or the lush valley
equally   fiercely

Birdwatching

I could move
        in and out of the cages
for they are unbirdened
        open and empty
(the words we said in each are flown)

Instead I sit in a cabin room
        fire blazing
and gaze through the window at bird life   free
to nip and tuck at the dangling flower-pot—

From a window it is easy to bird-watch
        from a closed-in thought
        not easy to catch
                        words flying
                words you had brushed from your mouth
                so carelessly
        that day we walked and talked in the summer wood
        when there was no cabin built
                its foundations our arms only
        pressing down last year's leaves.

The Eaters

i

My love
          so long spent
circling   hovering   blessing
has suddenly alighted
is pecking your heart
          (had you noticed)
Now you have been given
          the sign
now you are eaten
and I,   flown
circle the heavens
fanned by your flame

ii

I've swallowed you
through all my orifices
you are jonah'd now
fast
within me

iii

To toss the ball
is to pass oneself over
and returning
receive oneself
now again

Please   take my love
round
in your mouth

The Journey East

i

As I sit in my car
fast at the wheel
I feel you   within me
steering

How can I be blind
to
the light I move by?

ii

Riding along the freeway
into Quebec country
I toss quarters into the gaping
toll baskets
gladly

Riding back
it will not be the same:
they'll have to squeeze
each quarter out of me
drop
by
silver drop

iii

Patrouilles anonymes—
anonymous prowlers
search me

I was undressed
long before I ventured
onto the highway
They were right
to give me a ticket
You were right   also
to disown me

iv

SPEED LIMIT
            30
        SLOW
            curve
                HILL
                    falling
                        ROCK
DEER!
(the symbols multiply)
            going down hill
            the car
                    leaps like a mare
            heading for oats
            IT IS UNLAWFUL TO
                give her her head
            mine reels

                v

Having to come
            to this dreamed place
alone   the opposite ocean
I made the best of it:
when I chewed clam chowder
                I was nibbling your fingers
when I swallowed baked lobster whole
it was your forked tongue stabbing
when I went out after dark
along the esplanade at Saint Andrews
            a fine rain falling
I sucked sea salt into my lungs
            rubbed salt out of my eyes

vi

On the beach
the hot dog stand's
            enclosed in barbed wire
tables stacked
steel swings padlocked

In this motel
I end up chained
            to a wire bed
barbed bones screeching

vii

I force sleep
down my throat
stuff it into my lungs

The river also
at Fundy
seizes the sea
swallows that whale's belly
into its maw
and sleeps
curdled in its roar.

Another Journey

i

Now you have released me
from your grip
now I can slip   alone
into the forest

rest
upon stone

ii

A switchback trail
returns
    almost upon itself
then flicks its tail
against the flank
of yesterday

iii

I climb
    stolidly
looking neither right
    nor upward
in the dust
I see
wing swoops
    (hawk   shadow)
following me

iv

A path curls
a rope loops
a cracked whip
scoops a corner

    signals
        sparkle

v

Night
spills stars
into the valley

I am aware
of cedars   breathing
turning
the trees   move with me
        up   the mountain

The Operation

And I too
after the blaze of being   alive
faced the wall
over which breath must be thrown

faced the wall
scratched by the graffiti   of trying
and made there
my trembling mark

Where the knife was poised
a warm flame leaped   between us
I   victim
grateful to be saved
and he   appraising
how to create from bone and flesh
a new woman?
the needle shot into my arm
and I was his

In the dazed days that followed
he used to appear
in silent white precision
at my door
and stand there till I recognized
him   surgeon—
a nod: he waited with pursed lips
eyes quizzical beneath the furry brows
until I raged and ranted—
or docile on blue mornings
acknowledged all
solicitudes—
between us still
that intimate   flashing bond

Now it is over!   He pronounces health
I walk   near steady
out of his office   down his corridor
(the elevator sighs
the breath I fought for)
outside   pale
the autumn smog   the foul
snarl of commuting cars
the pavement's glare:
I have to breathe deep   here
to be alive again

2

You pulled me back
into life
your very penis   forging
pulling
me   back
refrain   refrain
love me again
and when once
was all I gasped for
(still in pain)
you demanded more:
love me again!

The second time I turned
swam with you into darkness
was the foetus
fed by blood
and breath
fighting to grow
gasping for air
world's door
—then drowned
and slept.

It is enough
I dreamed
but you
were ever again   there
over me   lord
over me cutting me open again
till the wound cried
and you took my pain into your side
and lay there   healing me
with gentle breath and tongue
lulling me down
tender   rocking   ease
and a quick come.

3

Later   the seasons came
and changed
this loving was a sickness   too
in which we said farewell
so many times
and each goodbye a prelude   prescope
        of the next
swung needles deeper into flesh
        split the mind's peace
Listen!   when rain rattles the branches
        our ghost shivers

(a kind of disease between us
        love was
indulged in as excuse
        for going to bed
we transmitted kisses
and I caught between my thighs
        the antibody)

From my convalescent window
I see you cured
jay-walking on robson street
        a well man
                free of opposites

it's cloudy still
rain
smirches the pane

Morning: I face
wet pavement   distorted
mirrors
            (green Christmas and your lean body
            lounging along the shore
            your lunging arms
            flung against boulders)

I decide to complete the operation
tear myself into four quarters
scatter the pieces
north
a crystal city of ice
arching up   stretching out daily
dazedly
into uncoiling
animal sun—
another kingdom

4

Until I'd found a doorway
I could stand in   push against
I did not know how shrunk
I had become
for now the *he*   the *you*   are one
and gone
and I must measure me

O let me grow
and push
upright!
ever aware of height
and the cry
to reach a dazzled strangeness
sun-pierced sky

The Pied Piper of Edmonton

i

O glitter city
my tongue licks up
your licorice
I swallow cars
and black tar strips
I suck a licorice whip
and conjure horses
flying above the highrises
galloping into cloud—

> *Lucy in the sky*
> *with diamonds*

all earth is OIL   OIL   OIL
and city lights devour the stars!
in sky
no diadem
no diamonds

ii

A shivering   Canadian flag
is sucked   every which way
by wind
its fiery leaf
blanched

three chimneys from the
city powerhouse
blast stinking breath
into pure sky:
below, their excrement
stirs ice
to muddy movement
in the coiled river

around about Garneau
white frame houses totter down
to rubble
replaced in their gaping cellars
by plugged-in cars

iii

I see the houses
obsolete as horses
champing at their bits
pulling at their reins
soon to take off

I see them shaking loose
from underpinnings
running at a gallop
along asphalt roads
and up   so gently
tilting
this way   that way
UP
to blue excitement
streamered sky

    from those glittering windows
    the last children wave
    they wave goodbye

iv

"The taxi's on me."
Shambling out of the Queen's Hotel
beer parlour.
And he steered the woman's hulk with long black hair
crazily walking
"This way."

His face, though—
  lean ascetic   fierce
  the face of Poundmaker
    leaning down from the saddle
      to give an order

"The taxi's on me."

    And he rode off
      in the general direction
        of Cutknife Hill

      v

Each year the birds come back
the cedar waxwings
seeking familiar landmarks
each year they lose again
to torn-up terri-
tory
excavated caves
on which are built
the human zoos
floor on terraced
floor

each year   each spring
I hear
the sparrows jittering
the magpies shriek
caught in a closed
playpen of smog and soot

each year we turn
the bright world inside out—
they fly to the old familiar tree
and crash their wings
against a cement phallus.

Canadiana

My grandmother's house in Winnipeg
stood opposite Luxton School
yellow-brick
solid as Victoria herself.
The roaring children
terrified my tremulous
protected childhood
and I came home from class
with nits in my hair
and a vision of small brutes
throwing tin cans
shouting "Yid! Yid!"
at my mother's best friend's
Jewish son.

Today in my old years
protected by knowledge
I take up lodgings in Edmonton
opposite a red brick school
solid   Victorian
with battlemented turret.
On the sloping lawns
a sign
KEEP OFF THE GRASS.
Luckily they do NOT
but roll on it
play cowboys   Indians
and when the first snow falls
softly softly
cloaking the school yard
they leap and slide
on these small slopes—
the closest they may ever come
to flying.

But today
there are no tin cans flung
in Edmonton.
It is a clean place, square
and multi-racial
                    (except when it comes
                        to Indians and Métis.)

Where I Usually Sit

Where I usually sit
is by the south window
with the sun
pouring in   over me
and the magenta
cyclamen   with dark green
hearts   for leaves
beside me   on the table.

The school is opposite.
Where I usually sit
is full of children
            flying on ice
sliding from the grim green door
zut! into the street
or along the low rail fence
loaded with snow
turning somersaults   in winter.

Where I usually sit
there are rowans   clustered
            with red berries
frosted with snow
and a magpie   zooming
from branch to branch

the traffic churns
on deserts of uncleared roadway
turning the white
to smudge.

Here at this window
I toss words back and forth
on the typewriter
I yearn
for friends and loves   far off
warmed by the coastal waters
I sorrow   a little
that I'm only an aging person
onlooker
petrified   behind glass

And yet
from where I usually sit
my feet slide and skate
my arms   gesticulate. . .
I stay in love with movement
hug   hug
the dancers
this world's youngest
most daring   dancers.

Seashelter

The houses last longer
than those who lived there
who hammered 2 by 4's
wainscotted, plastered walls
unfrantically
painted them pink or blue
(never a green wall)

This shingle house was made
high on a mountain
                  when the crew went in
to heave and haul
            the forest
tame it down
with donkey engine
then the stripped bark
and logs rolled
lumbering   down
             (the land left bleeding)

When they cleared out they hoisted houses high
on sledges over barren forest rubble
and tumbled them to the sea
to be towed down to the quiet beaches
Porpoise Bay
and landed.

House weather-stained
with leaking roof
     wind-beaten
       water-soaked
house lived in
       locked box where
I saw your faded photograph
in an old trunk

The cracking walls
still stood—
but you
had gone.

House amongst Trees

It's the stillness
no excitement
calm expression   upward
into sun   or cloud
no dismay
on a dark day
no demands made
to the sky

it's the quiet
lighting on
dark branches
no wind   or else
a sudden ruffle
from the sea
and tossing trees
obeying whatever will
is there
expectant   accepting
no more demanding than
the day itself asks
creeping under
a dark shield of leaves.

The Artefacts: West Coast

i

In the middle of the night
I hear this old house breathing
a steady sigh
when oak trees and rock shadows
assemble silence
under a high
white moon

I hear the old house turn
in its sleep
shifting the weight of long dead footsteps
from one wall to another
echoing the children's voices
shrilly calling
from one room to the next
repeating those whispers in the master bedroom
a cry, a long sigh of breath
from one body to another
when the holy ghost takes over

In the middle of the night
I wake
and hear time speaking

ii

History the young say
doesn't make sense
and what can I say
in rejoinder?

The history of this house
if explored
is perhaps only reiterated pattern
being made over and over
by the young, now—
so there's nothing gained or lost
from the not-knowing
from the non-pattern?

First it was forest; rock;
hidden ups and downs
a hill where oaks and pines
struggled
and if a stranger climbed
the topmost pine
he'd see the ocean flattening the mountains
the forest, serried—
below, only the sculpted bays
native encampments
ceremonial lodges, totem poles
and winter dances
the Raven overall
giver-of-light, supervising
and the white whale imminent
evil lurking
to be appeased with ritual
long hair dancing
feathered masks

And today
at Wreck Bay, Long Beach
the long hairs dance
shaking their necklaces
they do not paint their faces
nor wear masks
are vulnerable to the whale
unprotected think to find safety
in nakedness

(in the cities
the young are wiser
stave off the whale's power
with maxi-minis, fringes, tokens, charms
LONG HAIR)

but history begins
                        the woman said
when you are thirty
that tomtom, time
begins to beat
to beat for you

                    iii

And in this house, look
examine the door lintels
striated cleverly and crowned
by the encircled eye:
egg-and-dart

examine out of doors
those arabesques, supporting eaves
leaves leaves entwined
those shingled sidewalls
scalloped leaf imprinted
over leaf; the forest
pattern brought to shape the house;
and turrets high!   and branching rooms
and eaves where swallows nest.

And in this city on the brink
of forest—sea—
history delights that Queen Victoria
made marriage with the totem wilderness
the cedar silences
the raven's wing

iv

Now ravens build here still
Seagulls spiral
the hippie children in these attics
breathe and cry
unwittingly
the names of history
tumble from their lips:
Nootka   Nanaimo
Masset   Ucluelet
The map leaps up
            here did I live
                was born and reared
                here died

So: Chief Maquinna   Jewitt   Emily Carr

The map leaps up
from namelessness
to history
each place made ceremonial
when named
and its name
peopled!
events shouted!

            here the waters divided
            here the whale bellowed

v

In the middle of the night
the house heaves, unmoored
launched on a vast sea.

Rowan   Red Rowan

All my tears have turned to ice
winter enclosed   crystal
pale mouth   stiff
and the smile   frozen

If I walk in the snow's yard
fir arms laden
a few bright berries storm my eyes
rowan   red rowan

If I pause by a bare tree
snow down shaken
the jewelled jay and the chickadee
are less forsaken

I cannot cry till the far green time
when the hills loosen
and the tears in streams rove through my veins
into frenzied blossom

The Snow Girl's Ballad

I should have let you lay me in the snow
then lift me back
so that my body's trace
might still be there
come spring
a power in the grass
my bones
firing the stones
my eyes
anemones

O brightly would I lie
the body that you traced
with your fine fingers
the gaze entranced
from my garden place
up to your story windows

I should have let you know
more things about me
and never let you find
a world within
without me.

April

A thousand roots
combined to make this tulip
yet its identity is never the same
as last year's
              (pressing the petals back
                to search the centre)

never the same—nor you, nor I
never the same returning to this earth
mingling our roots
to make new colour
              (not so orange this year
                but pinkish red
                a longer stem, a more blown-outward
                flourish

              to bugle the sun)

De-Evolution

Bi-sexual, we
the human kind
cannot procreate
alone

but flower, plant
without a meeting
greets only the light
and is made quick

> Shall animal man
> searching the universe
> return   radiant
> self-creating?

> the thing
> in itself

Latter Day Eve

But supposing (only supposing)
it was God himself, not Satan
who held up the forbidden fruit
above her vision
(and not an apple—the biblical "fruit"—
but a cluster of cherries?)
He, an old roué, lusting
held up over her head
the glowing cherries
and it was Adam
young, virile, eager
who plucked one, swiftly
and popped it into her mouth.
Ah, sweetness!
the sweetness of ripe cherry.

When they were ushered out
into a world of teeming traffic
demolition deluge
cranes screeching
scaffolds folding
yellow caterpillars churning up
the lost
the last dimension
she glued herself to a telephone pole
and panicked, hoarsely:
where are you,
Adam?
Adam, where are you?

At the motel desk
she held up her room-key
so he would surely
see
but his eyes gazed steadily past her
at some disappearing waitress
and she flashed the key
fruitlessly!

Look to the End*

And if I hurt my knee
my good leg shows my poor leg
what to do

and if I hurt my arm
my good arm rubs my poor arm
into place

and if I hurt an eye
my good eye sees beyond the other's range
and pulls it onward   upward
into space

*respice ad finem, the Livesay motto

347

The sun's eye warms my heart
but if my good heart breaks
I have no twin
to make it beat again

Heritage

i

My father lived lusty but fearful
I am lusty and fearful

My father spoke his mind
sharply
I am sharp

He wrestled to lay the truth
and found her hard going
and sometimes he stumbled on stones
and turned by the wayside
and drank himself
maudlin

Sometimes I drink too—
too much
and sleep it off
in stony dreams

My father died
a sick, unhappy man—
let me die sooner!
not in bed, like him

but walking   running
leaping in the sun

ii

My father's crest
    is the lion's gamb
I wear his ring
    ask who I am

Aware so quickly
    of the burdened body
shrivelling eyes
    withered chin

Yet alive!   to move with the dancer
    stamping within—
he sets me down softly
    on the lion's skin.

The Children's Letters

They are my secret food
consumed in the most hushed corners
of my room
when no one's looking
I hold them up to sunlight
at the window
to see aright
to hear behind the spindly words
a child's tentative
                    first footsteps
a small voice stuttering
                    at the sky
"bird. . . bird. . ."

Whether these be
my children or my grandchildren
they're ghostly visitors
food of a solitary kind—
they leap on shafts of sunlight
through the mind's
shutters.

Waking in the Dark

Whenever I see him
in mind's eye
I see him light-haired and laughing
running in a green field

But day comes
radio is turned on
newspaper is insinuated
under the door
and there   between comic strips
ads   and girdled girls
black words mushroom:

It's going to take a hundred years
the experts say
to finish this genocide
a hundred years to annihilate a people
to bitter the ricefields with blood
dry Delta's water into salt—
a hundred years
so our grandchildren growing up
and their children
will be humans who feel no pity
for the green earth
and who look upon procreation
with indifference

When I see my grandchild running
in a game of football
his helmet is empty
in his right arm
he carries his head.

The Halloweens

i

The children have taken my bell!
just a small brass bell
from India
hung on the door lintel
to signal
some friend's arrival
    (as if they had taken a book
      or some poems
      and thrown them into the ditch)
the children have taken my bell

ii

I remember being twelve years old
wearing a black mask
over my eyes
a witch's cloak
over my shoulders
walking along Bloor St. with my sister
crying in the grocers' doorways
"Shell out! Shell out!
Halloween apples!"

iii

I remember the hard darkness
of teenage Halloween parties
when my mother dressed me
in an authentic Ukrainian costume
(borrowed from a dancer)
to be greeted with:
"The girls are all dressed as ghosts—
wouldn't you like a sheet?"
And shamefully
I let them re-dress me
in a sheet.

Late, late
cried bitterly
on the lone pillow
for the gay Ukrainian skirt
and my mother's wilful
short-sighted love.

iv

I remember my own small ones
in a deluge of rain, Vancouver
being shepherded in their drooping costumes
on their first "Halloween Handout"
and the shopping bags full of soggy
peanuts and apples—
never eaten

v

O yes I remember
Halloweens and Halloweens
(a quaint Canadian custom)
and the chance
             once every year
to act out the fantasy
overturn garbage pails
             in the witchwoman's garden
and to steal brass bells
(not meaning to steal them)
only wanting
to hear them   bell over bell
ringing   ringing
the wordless song

Weather Forecast

O what a horn
   blowing defeat
      through the bare limbs
         of trees

Tenderly
I gather a few delicate
     leaf shells
to carry into the house
for safety

It's the sixtieth year
of my life
and I discern
that spring is still
a verifiable
possibility!

Easter Saturday
for Georgia Ringrose, born Easter Dawn, 1971

A cold Easter
cold as Christmas—
raw wind
blisters of ice on grass
snow leeching
onto the lilac buds

     Is it that
     someone else is trying to enter
       in
           me
     and I keep closing the door?
     I lean against the door
     panting

a crack
a crack of sunlight
on the floor
dawn's whistle

I must wake up
must keep waking up

Let the door be
open
let the light of that new face
in

persuade yourself
to be two now
new now
within

tomorrow the stone
will be rolled away
utterly

we come out of the cave
two
in one

Disasters of the Sun
(1971)

Disasters of the Sun

i

O you old
gold garnered
incredible sun
sink through my skin
into the barren bone

If I'm real
I'm totem carved
with your splayed
scalpel

If I'm a person
the gods roar
in horrible surprised
masculinity

but if I'm a woman
paint me
with the beast   stripes
assure me I am human

ii

The world is round
it is an arm
a round us
my fingers touching Africa
your hand
tilting Siberian trees
our thoughts
still as the tundra stones
awaiting footprints

bright between our bones
shines the invisible sun

Though I was certain
we recognized each other
I could not speak:
the flashing fire
between us
fanned no words

In the airport circle   where
the baggage tumbled
all my jumbled life
fumbled
to find the one sweet piece
the clothing stuffed and duffled
labelled mine

and over across the circle saw
your dark hair, piercing eyes
lean profile, pipe in mouth.

      Incredibly, you move.
      You seem to dance
      and suddenly
      you stand beside me, calm
      without surprise:

      I cannot tell
      what country you are from
      we recognize each other
      and are dumb

      your hand   your hand
      tense on your pipe
      your look   *a soft bomb*
      behind my eyes

iv

My hands that used to be leaves
tender and sweet and soothing
have become roots
gnarled in soil

my hands
tender as green leaves
blowing on your skin
pulling you up
into joyous air
are knotted bones
whitening in the sun

v

During the last heat wave
a sunflower
that had stood up straight
outstaring the June
sun
wilted   collapsed
under a pitiless July
sky

now in burning August
I close out the city
trembling under heat
the green trees visibly
paling—

I close and curtain off myself
into four walls
breezed by a fan
but the fan
fumes!
and suddenly it
BREAKS OFF   from the wall
whirls   across the room
to rip my forefinger.

I tell you
we live in constant
danger
under the sun   bleeding
I tell you

vi

Keep out
keep out of the way of
this most killing
northern sun
grower   destroyer

Sun, you are no goodfather
but tyrannical king:
I have lived sixty years
under your fiery blades
all I want now
is to grope for those blunt
moon scissors

vii

When the black sun's
gone down
connect me underground:
root tentacles
subterranean water

no more lovely man can be
than he with moon-wand
who witches water

Index